Readings in the His
of Christian Theology

Volume 1

Books by William C. Placher
Published by The Westminster Press

Readings in the History of Christian Theology, Volume 1:
From Its Beginnings to the Eve of the Reformation

Readings in the History of Christian Theology, Volume 2:
From the Reformation to the Present

A History of Christian Theology: An Introduction

Readings in the History of Christian Theology

Volume 1

From Its Beginnings to the Eve
of the Reformation

William C. Placher

The Westminster Press
Philadelphia

Scripture quotations from the Revised Standard Version of the Bible are copyrighted 1946, 1952, © 1971, 1973 by the Division of Christian Education of the National Council of the Churches of Christ in the U.S.A. and are used by permission.

Book design by Gene Harris

First edition

Published by The Westminster Press®
Philadelphia, Pennsylvania

PRINTED IN THE UNITED STATES OF AMERICA

9 8 7 6

*These volumes are dedicated
to my mother,
in gratitude for a lifetime
of friendship, understanding,
and love*

Library of Congress Cataloging-in-Publication Data

Readings in the history of Christian theology / [edited by] William C. Placher. — 1st ed.
    p.   cm.
  Bibliography: p.
  Contents: v. 1. From its beginnings to the eve of the Reformation
— v. 2. From the Reformation to the present.
  ISBN 0-664-24057-7 (pbk. : v. 1).
  ISBN 0-664-24058-5 (pbk. : v. 2)

  1. Theology. I. Placher, William C. (William Carl), 1948–
BT80.R35 1988
230—dc19   87-29540
                                                           CIP

Contents

Preface

In 1983 The Westminster Press published a book I had written called *A History of Christian Theology*. The book's reviewers have been kind, and sales have been good. I have been particularly pleased by the teachers and students who have thanked me for the help it gave them in teaching and learning theology's history.

That earlier book, however, had an obvious limitation: it presented its story primarily in my words, with my interpretations. As soon as possible, students of any kind of history should be reading primary texts for themselves and reaching their own interpretations. But that isn't always easy. One of the themes of my earlier book was that Christian theology has always been a pluralistic affair, but with the escalating price of books, it is difficult to put together an affordable collection of readings that captures that diversity. I hope these two volumes will help.

To cast modesty aside, I think I have succeeded beyond my expectations. I had expected to put together a book of readings that would need to function as a supplement to a narrative history—my own or someone else's. That certainly remains one possible use. But, rather to my surprise, I found it possible to put together excerpts that, with brief introductions, form a roughly coherent narrative and stand on their own as a history of Christian theology. Keeping in mind that they might be used independently, I have repeated some material from my earlier book in introductions and suggestions for further reading.

These volumes share some of the features of my earlier book: an ecumenical perspective, a commitment to representing the tradition's diversity, a focus on the history of ideas rather than institutional history. I have tried to choose selections long enough to give a sense of the writer's style and to make it clear that theology does not consist simply of unsupported assertions but involves arguments. I have sought to keep my own introductions and notes to a minimum, to make room for as much of the primary texts as possible. Occasionally I have substituted U.S. spellings for British. Teachers are sometimes tempted to leave out things that have become, for them, overly familiar—but even the most familiar texts are often new to a student. Therefore, while I hope that even those expert in the field will find a few unfamiliar passages here, I have tried not to leave out the obvious ones.

No anthology is ever really satisfactory. If I were more learned or more imaginative, I am sure this one would be better. We keep learning more about the past, and we keep asking new questions of it as new issues arise in the present. So history keeps going out of date. In compiling this anthology, I was particularly conscious that new insights in feminist scholarship raise questions about both the selection and the translation of texts. I wish I had been able to take them more into account.

I am grateful to James Heaney, a committed and courageous editor who encouraged and supported my earlier book, and to Cynthia Thompson, my helpful editor for these volumes. The Lilly Library of Wabash College and the Regenstein Library of the University of Chicago and their staffs helped me at many points. My emeritus colleague John Charles answered questions over coffee about everything from medieval history to Greek grammar. I am also grateful to James McCord and the Center of Theological Inquiry for providing me with a wonderful "home away from home" for a year during which the final stages of this project were completed. My colleagues, students, and friends at Wabash continue to be a community that nurtures me in many ways. Wabash faculty development funds and money from the Eric Dean Fund helped support my research. I am above all grateful to my two research assistants: for over a year, David Schulz did everything from typing to tracking down publishers, and David Kirtley provided invaluable assistance in the project's final stages. Without them, I am not sure either I or the book would have made it.

W.C.P.

CHAPTER 1

Gnosticism
and Its Opponents

The New Testament records the beginnings of Christian theology. Paul and the author of the Gospel of John were the first great Christian theologians; the debates between Jewish and Gentile Christians recorded in Acts and in Paul's letters produced Christianity's first major theological controversies. Since those first Christian texts are as accessible as the nearest Bible, however, this collection begins with the earliest surviving Christian writings from outside the New Testament—the first of them probably written about the same time as the latest New Testament texts.

There were many very different strands in earliest Christianity, and these first theologians struggled to define what was "orthodox" and what was "heresy." The answers emerged only gradually. Perhaps the most important early debate concerned Gnosticism. "Gnosis" means "wisdom," and the Gnostics claimed to teach secret wisdom concerning how the world and evil emerged from disorder among the divine powers and how, by understanding our true natures, we can free our souls from our bodies and return to our true origins. Gnosticism began independent of Christianity, but many Gnostics soon identified Christ with the Savior figure common to Gnostic myths. But they denied that Christ had had a real physical body, for they were convinced of the evil of physical things. Some New Testament passages (Colossians 2 and Johannine emphases on Christ's human body, for instance) seem already directed against Gnostic Christians, but the conflict reached its height in the second century.

Other controversies took shape about the same time. Around 150 in Rome a Christian named Marcion advocated a radical break with Jewish traditions. The God of the Old Testament, he said, was the imperfect creator of an imperfect world, and quite different from the unqualifiedly good Father of Jesus Christ, who sent his Son to rescue us from this creation. Jews and Christians simply worship two different Gods, and the Father of Christ is not responsible for the evil in a world he did not make.

In Asia Minor, about the same time, Montanus and his followers proclaimed that the Holy Spirit spoke directly through them in their prophecies, with an authority that could supersede the writings of the apostles or the teachings of church officials.

In the face of Gnostics, Marcionites, and Montanists, their opponents had to defend the church's beliefs and patterns of authority more clearly. Gradually they defined a "canon" of official New Testament texts. The authority of bishops provided a way of overruling Gnostic teachers and Montanist prophets. Christian theologians began to define more clearly what they believed about Christ—emphasizing his full humanity and how he saves us. A clearer definition of "orthodox" Christian faith was emerging.

From *The Gospel of Thomas*

Beginning in 1945 a collection of Gnostic texts was discovered near the Egyptian village of Nag Hammadi. Earlier students of Gnosticism had been largely dependent on reports from the Gnostics' opponents. To a much greater extent, we can now hear the Gnostics speak for themselves. The Gospel of Thomas, *written in Syria, Palestine, or Mesopotamia sometime in the second century, is one of the most interesting of the Nag Hammadi documents. Many of the sayings of Jesus it presents closely parallel passages from the New Testament Gospels, but others illustrate the Gnostic emphasis on a secret tradition known only to the elect—and hint at the complex Gnostic attitudes toward women.*

These are the secret sayings which the living Jesus spoke and which Didymos Judas Thomas wrote down.

(1) And he said, "Whoever finds the interpretation of these sayings will not experience death."

(2) Jesus said, "Let him who seeks continue seeking until he finds. When he finds, he will become troubled. When he becomes troubled, he will be astonished, and he will rule over the All."

(3) Jesus said, "If those who lead you say to you, 'See, the Kingdom is in the sky,' then the birds of the sky will precede you. If they say to you, 'It is in the sea,' then the fish will precede you. Rather, the Kingdom is inside of you, and it is outside of you. When you come to know yourselves, then you will become known, and you will realize that it is you who are the sons of the living Father. But if you will not know yourselves, you dwell in poverty and it is you who are that poverty." . . .

(13) Jesus said to His disciples, "Compare me to someone and tell Me whom I am like."

Simon Peter said to Him, "You are like a righteous angel."

Matthew said to Him, "You are like a wise philosopher."

Thomas said to Him, "Master, my mouth is wholly incapable of saying whom You are like."

Jesus said, "I am not your master. Because you have drunk, you have become intoxicated from the bubbling spring which I have measured out."

And He took him and withdrew and told him three things. When Thomas returned to his companions, they asked him, "What did Jesus say to you?"

Thomas said to them, "If I tell you one of the things which he told me, you will pick up stones and throw them at me; a fire will come out of the stones and burn you up." . . .

(50) Jesus said, "If they say to you, 'Where did you come from?' say to them, 'We came from the light, the place where the light came into being on its own accord and established [itself] and became manifest through their image.' If they say to you, 'Is it you?' say, 'We are its children, and we are the elect of the Living Father.' If they ask you, 'What is the sign of your Father in you?' say to them, 'It is movement and repose.' " . . .

(108) Jesus said, "He who will drink from My mouth will become like Me. I myself shall become he, and the things that are hidden will be revealed to him."

(109) Jesus said, "The Kingdom is like a man who had [hidden] treasure in his field without knowing it. And [after] he died, he left it to his son. The son did not know (about the treasure). He inherited the field and sold [it]. And the one who bought it went plowing and found the treasure. He began to lend money at interest to whomever he wished."

(110) Jesus said, "Whoever finds the world and becomes rich, let him renounce the world."

(111) Jesus said, "The heavens and the earth will be rolled up in your presence. And the one who lives from the Living One will not see death." Does not Jesus say, "Whoever finds himself is superior to the world"?

(112) Jesus said, "Woe to the flesh that depends on the soul; woe to the soul that depends on the flesh."

(113) His disciples said to Him, "When will the Kingdom come?"

[Jesus said,] "It will not come by waiting for it. It will not be a matter of saying 'Here it is' or 'There it is.' Rather, the Kingdom of the Father is spread out upon the earth, and men do not see it."

(114) Simon Peter said to them, "Let Mary leave us, for women are not worthy of Life."

Jesus said, "I myself shall lead her in order to make her male, so that she too may become a living spirit resembling you males. For every woman who will make herself male will enter the Kingdom of Heaven."

Translated by Helmut Koester and Thomas O. Lambdin. From *The Nag Hammadi Library,* edited by James M. Robinson, pages 118–119, 123, 129–130. Copyright © 1978 by E. J. Brill. Reprinted by permission of E. J. Brill and Harper & Row, Publishers, Inc.

From *The Second Treatise of the Great Seth*

When and where this Nag Hammadi text was written remain unclear, but it certainly presents Gnostic ideas, including Docetism—the denial of Christ's real humanity. According to this selection, the Savior entered a human body but remained somehow quite distinct from that body, and Simon of Cyrene not only carried Jesus' cross [Matt. 27:32; Mark 15:21; Luke 23:26] but also died on it in Jesus' place. The text also refers to a number of the spiritual powers common in the complex Gnostic systems.

I visited a bodily dwelling. I cast out the one who was in it first, and I went in. And the whole multitude of the archons became troubled. And all the matter of the archons as well as all the begotten powers of the earth were shaken when it saw the likeness of the Image, since it was mixed. And I am the one who was in it, not resembling him who was in it first. For he was an earthly man, but I, I am from above the heavens. I did not refuse them even to become a Christ, but I did not reveal myself to them in the love which was coming forth from me. I revealed that I am a stranger to the regions below. . . .

And there came about a disturbance and a fight around the Seraphim and Cherubim since their glory will fade, and the confusion around Adonaios on both sides and their dwelling—to the Cosmocrator and him who said, "Let us seize him"; others again, "The plan will certainly not materialize." For Adonaios knows me because of hope. And I was in the mouths of lions. And the plan which they devised about me to release their error and their senselessness—I did not succumb to them as they had planned. But I was not afflicted at all. Those who were there punished me. And I did not die in reality but in appearance, lest I be put to shame by them because these are my kinsfolk. I removed the shame from me and I did not become fainthearted in the face of what happened to me at their hands. I was about to succumb to fear, and I <suffered> according to their sight and thought, in order that they may never find any word to speak about them. For my death which they think happened, (happened) to them in their error and blindness, since they nailed their man unto their death. For their Ennoias did not see me, for they were deaf and blind. But in doing these things, they condemn themselves. Yes, they saw me; they punished me. It was another, their father, who drank the gall and the vinegar; it was not I. They struck me with the reed; it was another, Simon, who bore the cross on his shoulder. It was another upon whom they placed the crown of thorns. But I was rejoicing in the height over all the wealth of the archons and the offspring of their error, of their empty glory. And I was laughing at their ignorance.

Translated by Joseph A. Gibbons, Roger A. Bullard, and Frederik Wisse. From *The Nag Hammadi Library,* edited by James M. Robinson, pages 330–332. Copyright © 1978 by E. J. Brill. Reprinted by permission of E. J. Brill and Harper & Row, Publishers, Inc.

Ignatius of Antioch (d. c.110)

From *Letter to the Trallians*

Ignatius, the bishop of Antioch in Syria and a great opponent of the Gnostics, was arrested for his Christian faith and led off to his death in Rome about 110. On the way from Syria to Rome, under arrest and facing death, he wrote a number of letters to Christian churches in the regions through which he traveled, urging faithfulness to their bishops and belief in Christ's real humanity.

1. Well do I realize what a character you have—above reproach and steady under strain. It is not just affected, but it comes naturally to you, as I gathered from Polybius, your bishop. By God's will and that of Jesus Christ, he came to me in Smyrna, and so heartily congratulated me on being a prisoner for Jesus Christ that in him I

saw your whole congregation. I welcomed, then, your good will, which reached me by him, and I gave thanks that I found you, as I heard, to be following God.

2. For when you obey the bishop as if he were Jesus Christ, you are (as I see it) living not in a merely human fashion but in Jesus Christ's way, who for our sakes suffered death that you might believe in his death and so escape dying yourselves. It is essential, therefore, to act in no way without the bishop, just as you are doing. Rather submit even to the presbytery as to the apostles of Jesus Christ. He is our Hope [cf. 1 Tim. 1:1], and if we live in union with him now, we shall gain eternal life. . . .

6. I urge you, therefore—not I, but Jesus Christ's love—use only Christian food. Keep off foreign fare, by which I mean heresy. For those people mingle Jesus Christ with their teachings just to gain your confidence under false pretenses. It is as if they were giving a deadly poison mixed with honey and wine, with the result that the unsuspecting victim gladly accepts it and drinks down death with fatal pleasure.

7. Be on your guard, then, against such people. This you will do by not being puffed up and by keeping very close to [our] God, Jesus Christ, and the bishop and the apostles' precepts. Inside the sanctuary a man is pure; outside he is impure. That means: whoever does anything without the bishop, presbytery, and deacons does not have a clear conscience.

8. It is not because I have heard of any such thing in your case that I write thus. No, in my love for you I am warning you ahead, since I foresee the devil's wiles. Recapture, then, your gentleness, and by faith (that's the Lord's flesh) and by love (that's Jesus Christ's blood) make yourselves new creatures. Let none of you hold anything against his neighbor. Do not give the heathen opportunities whereby God's people should be scoffed at through the stupidity of a few. For, "Woe to him by whose folly my name is scoffed at before any" [Isa. 52:5].

9. Be deaf, then, to any talk that ignores Jesus Christ, of David's lineage, of Mary; who was really born, ate, and drank; was really persecuted under Pontius Pilate; was really crucified and died, in the sight of heaven and earth and the underworld. He was really raised from the dead, for his Father raised him, just as his Father will raise us, who believe on him, through Christ Jesus, apart from whom we have no genuine life.

10. And if, as some atheists (I mean unbelievers) say, his suffering

was a sham (it's really *they* who are a sham!), why, then, am I a prisoner? Why do I want to fight with wild beasts? In that case I shall die to no purpose. Yes, and I am maligning the Lord too!

From *Early Christian Fathers,* edited and translated by Cyril C. Richardson (Volume I: The Library of Christian Classics), pages 98–100. First published in MCMLIII by the SCM Press Ltd., London, and The Westminster Press, Philadelphia. Used by permission of the publishers.

Ignatius of Antioch

From *Letter to the Romans*

Ignatius feared that Christians in Rome might try to arrange his escape; he wrote ahead to assure them of his willingness to die for his faith.

4. I am corresponding with all the churches and bidding them all realize that I am voluntarily dying for God—if, that is, you do not interfere. I plead with you, do not do me an unseasonable kindness. Let me be fodder for wild beasts—that is how I can get to God. I am God's wheat and I am being ground by the teeth of wild beasts to make a pure loaf for Christ. I would rather that you fawn on the beasts so that they may be my tomb and no scrap of my body be left. Thus, when I have fallen asleep, I shall be a burden to no one. Then I shall be a real disciple of Jesus Christ when the world sees my body no more. Pray Christ for me that by these means I may become God's sacrifice. I do not give orders like Peter and Paul. They were apostles: I am a convict. They were at liberty: I am still a slave [Cf. 1 Cor. 7:22]. But if I suffer, I shall be emancipated by Jesus Christ; and united to him, I shall rise to freedom.

5. Even now as a prisoner, I am learning to forego my own wishes. All the way from Syria to Rome I am fighting with wild beasts, by land and sea, night and day, chained as I am to ten leopards (I mean to a detachment of soldiers), who only get worse the better you treat them. But by their injustices I am becoming a better disciple, "though not for that reason am I acquitted" [1 Cor. 4:4]. What a thrill I shall have from the wild beasts that are ready for me! I hope they will make short work of me. I shall coax them on to eat me up at once and not to hold off, as sometimes happens, through fear. And if they are reluctant, I shall force them to it. Forgive me—I know

what is good for me. Now is the moment I am beginning to be a
disciple. May nothing seen or unseen begrudge me making my way
to Jesus Christ. Come fire, cross, battling with wild beasts, wrenching
of bones, mangling of limbs, crushing of my whole body, cruel tor-
tures of the devil—only let me get to Jesus Christ!

From *Early Christian Fathers,* edited and translated by Cyril C. Richardson (Vol-
ume I: The Library of Christian Classics), pages 104–105. First published in
MCMLIII by the SCM Press Ltd., London, and The Westminster Press,
Philadelphia. Used by permission of the publishers.

Irenaeus (c.140–c.202)

From *Against Heresies*

*Irenaeus was born in Asia Minor around 140 but moved to what is
now France, where he served as bishop of the city of Lyons until his
death around 202. His* Against Heresies *tried to summarize and
refute all the heresies he saw threatening the church. His summaries
remain a crucial source of information about his opponents. This
passage discusses the system of Ptolemaeus, an Egyptian Gnostic of the
late second century. As in many Gnostic theories, a large number of
divine powers or aeons separates the highest divinity from the creation
of the physical world. One of the lower aeons is Sophia, or Wisdom,
whose fall brought about the real beginning of evil.*

Book 1

Chapter 1. 1. They maintain, then, that in the invisible and ineffable heights above there exists a certain perfect, pre-existent Aeon,
whom they call Proarche, Propator, and Bythus and describe as
being invisible and incomprehensible. Eternal and unbegotten, he
remained throughout innumerable cycles of ages in profound serenity and quiescence. There existed along with him Ennoea, whom they
also call Charis and Sige. At last this Bythus determined to send
forth from himself the beginning of all things, and deposited this
production (which he had resolved to bring forth) in his contemporary Sige, even as seed is deposited in the womb. She then, having
received this seed, and becoming pregnant, gave birth to Nous, who
was both similar and equal to him who had produced him, and was
alone capable of comprehending his father's greatness. This Nous
they call also Monogenes, and Father, and the Beginning of all

Things. Along with him was also produced Aletheia; and these four constituted the first and first-begotten Pythagorean Tetrad, which they also denominate the root of all things. For there are first Bythus and Sige, and then Nous and Aletheia.

And Monogenes, perceiving for what purpose he had been produced, also himself sent forth Logos and Zoe, being the father of all those who were to come after him, and the beginning and fashioning of the entire Pleroma.* By the conjunction of Logos and Zoe were brought forth Anthropos and Ecclesia; and thus was formed the first-begotten Ogdoad, the root and substance of all things, called among them by four names, viz., Bythus, and Nous, and Logos, and Anthropos. For each of these is masculo-feminine, as follows: Propator was united by a conjunction with his Ennoea; then Monogenes, that is Nous, with Aletheia; Logos with Zoe, and Anthropos with Ecclesia. . . .

2. . . . Logos and Zoe, after producing Anthropos and Ecclesia, sent forth other ten Aeons, whose names are the following: Bythius and Mixis, Ageratos and Henosis, Autophyes and Hedone, Acinetos and Syncrasis, Monogenes and Macaria. These are the ten Aeons whom they declare to have been produced by Logos and Zoe. They then add that Anthropos himself, along with Ecclesia, produced twelve Aeons, to whom they give the following names: Paracletus and Pistis, Patricos and Elpis, Metricos and Agape, Ainos and Syesis, Ecclesiasticus and Macariotes, Theletos and Sophia. . . .

Chapter 2. 2. But there rushed forth in advance of the rest that Aeon who was much the latest of them, and was the youngest of the Duodecad† which sprang from Anthropos and Ecclesia, namely Sophia, and suffered passion apart from the embrace of her consort Theletos. This passion, indeed, first arose among those who were connected with Nous and Aletheia, but passed as by contagion to this degenerate Aeon, who acted under a pretence of love, but was in reality influenced by temerity, because she had not, like Nous, enjoyed communion with the perfect Father. This passion, they say, consisted in a desire to search into the nature of the Father; for she wished, according to them, to comprehend his greatness. When she could not attain her end, inasmuch as she aimed at an impossibility,

---

*The heavenly hierarchy of the aeons.

†The twelve aeons just mentioned.

and thus became involved in an extreme agony of mind, while both on account of the vast profundity as well as the unsearchable nature of the Father, and on account of the love she bore him, she was ever stretching herself forward, there was danger lest she should at last have been absorbed by his sweetness, and resolved into his absolute essence, unless she had met with that Power which supports all things, and preserves them outside of the unspeakable greatness. This power they term Horos;* by whom, they say, she was restrained and supported; and that then, having with difficulty been brought back to herself, she was convinced that the Father is incomprehensible. . . .

4. And by this Horos they declare that Sophia was purified and established, while she was also restored to her proper conjunction. For her enthymesis (or inborn idea) having been taken away from her, along with its supervening passion, she herself certainly remained within the Pleroma; but her enthymesis, with its passion, was separated from her by Horos, fenced off, and expelled from that circle. This enthymesis was, no doubt, a spiritual substance, possessing some of the natural tendencies of an Aeon, but at the same time shapeless and without form, because it had received nothing. And on this account they say that it was an imbecile and feminine production.

5. After this substance had been placed outside of the Pleroma of the Aeons, and its mother restored to her proper conjunction, they tell us that Monogenes, acting in accordance with the prudent forethought of the Father, gave origin to another conjugal pair, namely Christ and the Holy Spirit (lest any of the Aeons should fall into a calamity similar to that of Sophia), for the purpose of fortifying and strengthening the Pleroma, and who at the same time completed the number of the Aeons. . . .

Chapter 3. 1. Such, then, is the account they give of what took place within the Pleroma; such the calamities that flowed from the passion which seized upon the Aeon who has been named, and who was within a little of perishing by being absorbed in the universal substance, through her inquisitive searching after the Father; such the consolidation [of that Aeon] from her condition of agony by Horos, and Stauros, and Lytrotes, and Carpistes, and Horothetes, and Metagoges. Such also is the account of the generation of the later

---

*Limit.

Aeons, namely of the first Christ and of the Holy Spirit, both of whom were produced by the Father after the repentance [of Sophia], and of the second Christ (whom they also style Saviour), who owed his being to the joint contributions [of the Aeons]. They tell us, however, that this knowledge has not been openly divulged, because all are not capable of receiving it, but has been mystically revealed by the Saviour through means of parables to those qualified for understanding it.

From *The Ante-Nicene Fathers,* edited and translated by Alexander Roberts and James Donaldson (Buffalo: Christian Literature Company, 1884–1886), Volume 1, pages 316–319.

Eusebius (c.260–c.339)

From *Church History*

Eusebius was bishop of Caesarea in Syria and played an important role at the Council of Nicaea in 325, but he is best known for his history of the early church. His bias against the Montanists is obvious. This report was written over a century after Montanus began prophesying somewhere between 155 and 175, so it needs to be read with caution, but it still provides much of our best evidence about the beginnings of Montanism.

Book 5

Chapter 16. There is said to be a certain village called Ardabau in that part of Mysia, which borders upon Phrygia. There first, they say, when Gratus was proconsul of Asia, a recent convert, Montanus by name, through his unquenchable desire for leadership, gave the adversary opportunity against him. And he became beside himself, and being suddenly in a sort of frenzy and ecstasy, he raved, and began to babble and utter strange things, prophesying in a manner contrary to the constant custom of the Church handed down by tradition from the beginning. Some of those who heard his spurious utterances at that time were indignant, and they rebuked him as one that was possessed, and that was under the control of a demon, and was led by a deceitful spirit, and was distracting the multitude; and they forbade him to talk, remembering the distinction drawn by the Lord and his warning to guard watchfully against the coming of false prophets. But others imagining themselves possessed of the Holy Spirit and of a prophetic gift, were elated and not a little puffed up; and forgetting the distinction of the Lord, they challenged the mad and insidious and seducing spirit, and were cheated and deceived by him. In consequence of this, he could no longer be held in check, so as to keep silence. Thus by artifice, or rather by such a system of wicked craft, the devil, devising destruction for the disobedient, and being unworthily honored by them, secretly excited and inflamed their understandings which had already become estranged from the true faith. And he stirred up besides two women, and filled them with the false spirit, so that they talked wildly and unreasonably and strangely, like the person already mentioned. And the spirit pronounced them blessed as they rejoiced and gloried in him, and puffed them up by the magnitude of his promises. But sometimes he rebuked them openly in a wise and faithful manner, that he might seem to be a reprover. But those of the Phrygians that were deceived were few in number.

And the arrogant spirit taught them to revile the entire universal Church under heaven, because the spirit of false prophecy received neither the honor from it nor entrance into it. For the faithful in Asia met often in many places throughout Asia to consider this matter, and examined the novel utterances and pronounced them profane, and rejected the heresy, and thus these persons were expelled from the Church and debarred from communion.

Translated by Arthur Cushman McGiffert. From *The Nicene and Post-Nicene Fathers,* 2nd Series, edited by Philip Schaff and Henry Wace (New York: Christian Literature Company, 1890–1900), Volume 1, pages 231–232.

From *The Teaching of the Twelve Apostles*

A copy of this document was discovered in Constantinople in 1873. Its origin continues to be debated, but it seems likely to have come from somewhere in Syria, sometime in the second century. It apparently describes the customs of quite early Syrian Christians. It is not directed against Montanism as such, but it does show a caution about wandering prophets and the emphasis on order and established church leadership that characterized many responses to the Montanists. The Teaching *(or* Didache, *as it is called in Greek) also provides important information about the early theory and practice of the Eucharist and baptism.*

See "that no one leads you astray" [Matt. 24:4] from this way of the teaching, since such a one's teaching is godless.

If you can bear the Lord's full yoke, you will be perfect. But if you cannot, then do what you can.

Now about food: undertake what you can. But keep strictly away from what is offered to idols, for that implies worshiping dead gods.

Now about baptism: this is how to baptize. Give public instruction on all these points, and then "baptize" in running water, "in the name of the Father and of the Son and of the Holy Spirit" [Matt. 28:19]. If you do not have running water, baptize in some other. If you cannot in cold, then in warm. If you have neither, then pour water on the head three times "in the name of the Father, Son, and Holy Spirit" [Matt. 28:19]. Before the baptism, moreover, the one who baptizes and the one being baptized must fast, and any others who can. And you must tell the one being baptized to fast for one or two days beforehand. . . .

Now about the Eucharist: This is how to give thanks: First in connection with the cup:

"We thank you, our Father, for the holy vine of David, your child, which you have revealed through Jesus, your child. To you be glory forever."

Then in connection with the piece [broken off the loaf]:

"We thank you, our Father, for the life and knowledge which you have revealed through Jesus, your child. To you be glory forever.

"As this piece [of bread] was scattered over the hills and then was brought together and made one, so let your Church be brought together from the ends of the earth into your Kingdom. For yours is the glory and the power through Jesus Christ forever."

You must not let anyone eat or drink of your Eucharist except those baptized in the Lord's name. For in reference to this the Lord said, "Do not give what is sacred to the dogs" [Matt. 7:6]. . . .

Now, you should welcome anyone who comes your way and teaches you all we have been saying. But if the teacher proves himself a renegade and by teaching otherwise contradicts all this, pay no attention to him. But if his teaching furthers the Lord's righteousness and knowledge, welcome him as the Lord.

Now about the apostles and prophets: Act in line with the gospel precept. Welcome every apostle on arriving, as if he were the Lord. But he must not stay beyond one day. In case of necessity, however, the next day too. If he stays three days, he is a false prophet. On departing, an apostle must not accept anything save sufficient food to carry him till his next lodging. If he asks for money, he is a false prophet.

While a prophet is making ecstatic utterances, you must not test or examine him. For "every sin will be forgiven," but this sin "will not be forgiven" [Matt. 12:31]. However, not everybody making ecstatic utterances is a prophet, but only if he behaves like the Lord. It is by their conduct that the false prophet and the [true] prophet can be distinguished. For instance, if a prophet marks out a table in the Spirit, he must not eat from it. If he does, he is a false prophet. Again, every prophet who teaches the truth but fails to practice what he preaches is a false prophet. But every attested and genuine prophet who acts with a view to symbolizing the mystery of the Church, and does not teach you to do all he does, must not be judged by you. His judgment rests with God. For the ancient prophets too acted in this way. But if someone says in the Spirit, "Give me money, or something else," you must not heed him. However, if he tells you to give for others in need, no one must condemn him.

From *Early Christian Fathers,* edited and translated by Cyril C. Richardson (Volume I: The Library of Christian Classics), pages 174–177. First published in MCMLIII by the SCM Press Ltd., London, and The Westminster Press, Philadelphia. Used by permission of the publishers.

Irenaeus

From *Against Heresies*

Irenaeus is not only a good source of information about many early heresies; he was also important in developing the "orthodox" response to them. The following selections begin with his account of Marcion's views—his belief in two Gods and his edited version of the New Testament. Irenaeus then goes on to develop his own ideas about Scripture, tradition, and the church, in large part in response to Gnostic claims to a secret tradition of "perfect knowledge."

Book 1

Chapter 27. 2. Marcion of Pontus . . . advanced the most daring blasphemy against Him who is proclaimed as God by the law and the prophets, declaring Him to be the author of evils, to take delight in war, to be infirm of purpose, and even to be contrary to Himself.

But Jesus being derived from that father who is above the God that made the world, and coming into Judaea in the time of Pontius Pilate the governor, who was the procurator of Tiberius Caesar, was manifested in the form of a man to those who were in Judaea, abolishing the prophets and the law, and all the works of that God who made the world, whom also he calls Cosmocrator. Besides this, he mutilates the Gospel which is according to Luke, removing all that is written respecting the generation of the Lord, and setting aside a great deal of the teaching of the Lord, in which the Lord is recorded as most clearly confessing that the Maker of this universe is His Father. He likewise persuaded his disciples that he himself was more worthy of credit than are those apostles who have handed down the Gospel to us, furnishing them not with the Gospel, but merely a fragment of it. In like manner, too, he dismembered the Epistles of Paul, removing all that is said by the apostle respecting that God who made the world, to the effect that He is the Father of our Lord Jesus Christ, and also those passages from the prophetical writings which the apostle quotes, in order to teach us that they announced beforehand the coming of the Lord. . . .

Book 2

Chapter 25. 3. Marcion, therefore, himself, by dividing God into two, maintaining one to be good and the other judicial, does in fact, on both sides, put an end to deity. For he that is the judicial one, if he be not good, is not God, because he from whom goodness is absent is no God at all; and again, he who is good, if he has no judicial power, suffers the same [loss] as the former, by being deprived of his character of deity. . . .

Book 3

Chapter 1. 1. We have learned from none others the plan of our salvation, than from those through whom the Gospel has come down to us, which they did at one time proclaim in public, and, at a later period, by the will of God, handed down to us in the Scriptures, to be the ground and pillar of our faith. For it is unlawful to assert that they preached before they possessed "perfect knowledge," as some do even venture to say, boasting themselves as improvers of the apostles. For, after our Lord rose from the dead, [the apostles] were invested with power from on high when the Holy Spirit came down [upon them], were filled from all [His gifts], and had perfect knowledge: they departed to the ends of the earth, preaching the glad tidings of the good things [sent] from God to us, and proclaiming the peace of heaven to men, who indeed do all equally and individually possess the Gospel of God. Matthew also issued a written Gospel among the Hebrews in their own dialect, while Peter and Paul were preaching at Rome, and laying the foundations of the Church. After their departure, Mark, the disciple and interpreter of Peter, did also hand down to us in writing what had been preached by Peter. Luke also, the companion of Paul, recorded in a book the Gospel preached by him. Afterwards, John, the disciple of the Lord, who also had leaned upon His breast, did himself publish a Gospel during his residence at Ephesus in Asia. These have all declared to us that there is one God, Creator of heaven and earth, announced by the law and the prophets; and one Christ, the Son of God. If any one do not agree to these truths, he despises the companions of the Lord; nay more, he despises Christ Himself the Lord; yea, he despises the Father also, and stands self-condemned, resisting and opposing his own salvation, as is the case with all heretics. . . .

Chapter 2. 2. But, again, when we refer them to that tradition which originates from the apostles, [and] which is preserved by means of the successions of presbyters in the Churches, they object to tradition, saying that they themselves are wiser not merely than the presbyters, but even than the apostles, because they have discovered the unadulterated truth. . . .

Chapter 3. 1. It is within the power of all, therefore, in every Church, who may wish to see the truth, to contemplate clearly the tradition of the apostles manifested throughout the whole world; and we are in a position to reckon up those who were by the apostles instituted bishops in the Churches, and [to demonstrate] the succession of these men to our own times; those who neither taught nor knew of anything like what these [heretics] rave about. For if the apostles had known hidden mysteries, which they were in the habit of imparting to "the perfect" apart and privily from the rest, they would have delivered them especially to those to whom they were also committing the Churches themselves. For they were desirous that these men should be very perfect and blameless in all things, whom also they were leaving behind as their successors, delivering up their own place of government to these men; which men, if they discharged their functions honestly, would be a great boon [to the Church], but if they should fall away, the direst calamity.

2. Since, however, it would be very tedious, in such a volume as this, to reckon up the successions of all the Churches, we do put to confusion all those who, in whatever manner, whether by an evil self-pleasing, by vainglory, or by blindness and perverse opinion, assemble in unauthorized meetings; [we do this, I say,] by indicating that tradition derived from the apostles, of the very great, the very ancient, and universally known Church founded and organized at Rome by the two most glorious apostles, Peter and Paul; as also [by pointing out] the faith preached to men, which comes down to our time by means of the successions of the bishops. For it is a matter of necessity that every Church should agree with this Church, on account of its preeminent authority, that is, the faithful everywhere, inasmuch as the apostolical tradition has been preserved continuously by those [faithful men] who exist everywhere. . . .

Chapter 18. 6. . . . For if He did not truly suffer, no thanks to Him, since there was no suffering at all; and when we shall actually begin to suffer, He will seem as leading us astray, exhorting us to endure buffeting, and to turn the other cheek, if He did not Himself before us in reality suffer the same; and as He misled them by seeming to them what He was not, so does He also mislead us, by exhorting us to endure what He did not endure Himself. [In that case] we shall be even above the Master, because we suffer and sustain what our Master never bore or endured. But as our Lord is alone truly Master, so the Son of God is truly good and patient, the Word of God the Father having been made the Son of man. For he fought and conquered; for He was man contending for the fathers, and through obedience doing away with disobedience completely: for He bound the strong man, and set free the weak, and endowed His own handiwork with salvation, by destroying sin. For He is a most holy and merciful Lord, and loves the human race.

7. Therefore, as I have already said, He caused man (human nature) to cleave to and to become one with God. For unless man had overcome the enemy of man, the enemy would not have been legitimately vanquished. And again: unless it had been God who had freely given salvation, we could never have possessed it securely. And unless man had been joined to God, he could never have become a partaker of incorruptibility. For it was incumbent upon the Mediator between God and men, by His relationship to both, to bring both to

friendship and concord, and present man to God, while He revealed God to man. For, in what way could we be partakers of the adoption of sons, unless we had received from Him through the Son that fellowship which refers to Himself, unless His Word, having been made flesh, had entered into communion with us? Wherefore also He passed through every stage of life, restoring to all communion with God. Those, therefore, who assert that He appeared putatively, and was neither born in the flesh nor truly made man, are as yet under the old condemnation, holding out patronage to sin; for, by their showing, death has not been vanquished, which "reigned from Adam to Moses, even over them that had not sinned after the similitude of Adam's transgression" [Rom. 5:14]. But the law coming, which was given by Moses, and testifying of sin that it is a sinner, did truly take away his (death's) kingdom, showing that he was no king, but a robber; and it revealed him as a murderer. It laid, however, a weighty burden upon man, who had sin in himself, showing that he was liable to death. For as the law was spiritual, it merely made sin to stand out in relief, but did not destroy it. For sin had no dominion over the spirit, but over man. For it behooved Him who was to destroy sin, and redeem man under the power of death, that He should Himself be made that very same thing which he was, that is, man who had been drawn by sin into bondage, but was held by death, so that sin should be destroyed by man, and man should go forth from death. For as by the disobedience of the one man who was originally moulded from virgin soil, the many were made sinners, and forfeited life; so was it necessary that, by the obedience of one man, who was originally born from a virgin, many should be justified and receive salvation. Thus, then was the Word of God made man, as also Moses says: "God, true are His works" [Deut. 32:4]. But if, not having been made flesh, He did appear as if flesh, His work was not a true one. But what He did appear, that He also was: God recapitulated in Himself the ancient formation of man, that He might kill sin, deprive death of its power, and vivify man; and therefore His works are true.

Chapter 19. 1. But again, those who assert that He was simply a mere man, begotten by Joseph, remaining in the bondage of the old disobedience, are in a state of death; having been not as yet joined to the Word of God the Father, nor receiving liberty through the Son, as He does Himself declare: "If the Son shall make you free, ye shall be free indeed" [John 8:36]. But, being ignorant of Him who from the Virgin is Emmanuel, they are deprived of His gift, which is eternal life; and not receiving the incorruptible Word, they remain in mortal flesh, and are debtors to death, not obtaining the antidote of life. To whom the Word says, mentioning His own gift of grace: "I said, Ye are all the sons of the Highest, and gods; but ye shall die like men" [Ps. 82:6–7]. He speaks undoubtedly these words to those who have not received the gift of adoption, but who despise the incarnation of the pure generation of the Word of God, defraud human nature of promotion into God, and prove themselves ungrateful to the Word of God, who became flesh for them. For it was for this end that the Word of God was made man, and He who was the Son of God became the Son of man, that man, having been taken into the Word, and receiving the adoption, might become the son of God. For by no other means could we have attained to incorruptibility and immortality, unless we had been united to incorruptibility and immortality. But how could we be joined to incorruptibility and immortality, unless, first, incorruptibility and immortality had become that which we also are, so that the corruptible might be swallowed up by incorruptibility, and the mortal by immortality, that we might receive the adoption of sons?

From *The Ante-Nicene Fathers,* edited and translated by Alexander Roberts and James Donaldson (Buffalo: Christian Literature Company, 1884–1886), Volume 1, pages 352, 459, 414–416, 447–449.

CHAPTER 2

Apologists, the School of Alexandria, and Tertullian

The debates over Gnosticism, Marcion, and the Montanists took place within Christianity. Their opponents might attack these groups as heretics, but they were Christian heretics. But as it moved through the world of the Roman Empire, Christianity also faced debates with non-Christians. The "Apologists" advanced the Christian case in such debates. "Apology" means "a speech in defense" such as might be given in a trial; the Apologists often wrote to the emperor to defend Christians against the charges that led to their persecution. Popular slanders against Christians, they explained, were unfair. Christians were morally upright, honest citizens. Justin Martyr, one early Apologist, associated Christianity with the best of the classical philosophical tradition, in contrast to the immoral superstition he saw in pagan religion.

The Apologists sometimes had to defend Christianity against the charge that it appealed only to the ignorant lower classes. That was certainly not true in Alexandria in Egypt, where the conversion of educated people called for intellectual leadership that would relate Christianity to the wider culture on a sophisticated level. At the end of the second century, Clement of Alexandria led in that effort, teaching in a special school for more educated converts. A generation later, Origen combined philosophical sophistication with learned biblical interpretation. Origen stands as the first great Christian systematic theologian and as one of the most prolific biblical commentators in history, though his belief that everyone will eventually be saved and his emphasis on allegorical interpretation of the Bible soon became—and still remain—controversial.

Farther to the west in North Africa, at about the same time, Tertullian challenged even the idea of connecting Christian faith to classical philosophy. His Roman practical sense—he was the first major Christian author to write in Latin rather than Greek—led him to distrust philosophical speculation on principle. His style of "apologetics" defined Christianity in sharp opposition to the culture that surrounded it, as opposed to the more conciliatory approaches of Justin and the school of Alexandria.

Justin Martyr (d. c.165)

From *First Apology*

Justin was born in Palestine but taught first at Ephesus and then at Rome—though he still wrote in Greek. He died about 165, apparently as a martyr under the persecution of the time. His Apology *urged the emperor to reject unfair accusations made against Christians, such as the charge of atheism, which Justin noted had been made against Socrates too. In both cases, he said, the accusations had been instigated by "demons." In general, "daimon" in Greek could refer to any divine spirit, but Justin gave it a clearly negative meaning.*

1. To the Emperor Titus Aelius Adrianus Antoninus Pius Augustus Caesar, and to his son Verissimus the Philosopher, and to Lucius the Philosopher, the natural son of Caesar, and the adopted son of Pius, a lover of learning, and to the sacred Senate, with the whole People of the Romans, I, Justin, the son of Priscus and grandson of Bacchius, natives of Flavia Neapolis in Palestine, present this address and petition in behalf of those of all nations who are unjustly hated and wantonly abused, myself being one of them.

2. Reason directs those who are truly pious and philosophical to honor and love only what is true, declining to follow traditional opinions, if these be worthless. . . . Do you, then, since ye are called pious and philosophers, guardians of justice and lovers of learning, give good heed, and hearken to my address; and if ye are indeed such, it will be manifested. . . .

3. But lest any one think that this is an unreasonable and reckless utterance, we demand that the charges against the Christians be investigated, and that, if these be substantiated, they be punished as they deserve. . . .

5. . . . when Socrates endeavoured, by true reason and examination, to . . . deliver men from the demons, then the demons themselves, by means of men who rejoiced in iniquity, compassed his death, as an atheist and a profane person, on the charge that "he was introducing new divinities"; and in our case they display a similar

activity. For not only among the Greeks did reason (Logos) prevail to condemn these things through Socrates, but also among the Barbarians were they condemned by Reason (or the Word, the Logos) Himself, who took shape, and became man, and was called Jesus Christ; and in obedience to Him, we not only deny that they who did such things as these are gods, but assert that they are wicked and impious demons, whose actions will not bear comparison with those even of men desirous of virtue.

6. Hence are we called atheists. And we confess that we are atheists, so far as gods of this sort are concerned, but not with respect to the most true God, the Father of righteousness and temperance and the other virtues, who is free from all impurity. But both Him, and the Son (who came forth from Him and taught us these things, and the host of the other good angels who follow and are made like to Him), and the prophetic Spirit, we worship and adore, knowing them in reason and truth, and declaring without grudging to every one who wishes to learn, as we have been taught. . . .

13. What sober-minded man, then, will not acknowledge that we are not atheists, worshipping as we do the Maker of this universe, and declaring, as we have been taught, that He has no need of streams of blood and libations and incense; whom we praise to the utmost of our power by the exercise of prayer and thanksgiving for all things wherewith we are supplied, as we have been taught that the only honor that is worthy of Him is not to consume by fire what He has brought into being for our sustenance, but to use it for ourselves and those who need, and with gratitude to Him to offer thanks by invocations and hymns for our creation, and for all the means of health, and for the various qualities of the different kinds of things, and for the changes of the seasons; and to present before Him petitions for our existing again in incorruption through faith in Him. Our teacher of these things is Jesus Christ, who also was born for this purpose, and was crucified under Pontius Pilate, procurator of Judaea, in the times of Tiberius Caesar; and that we reasonably worship Him, having learned that He is the Son of the true God Himself, and holding Him in the second place, and the prophetic Spirit in the third, we will prove. For they proclaim our madness to consist in this, that we give to a crucified man a place second to the unchangeable and eternal God, the Creator of all; for they do not discern the mystery that is herein, to which, as we make it plain to you, we pray you to give heed.

From *The Ante-Nicene Fathers,* edited and translated by Alexander Roberts and James Donaldson (Christian Literature Company, 1884–1886), Volume 1, pages 163–164, 166, 183–185.

Clement of Alexandria (d. c.210)

From *Exhortation to the Heathen*

Clement was born in the middle of the second century and died sometime after 210. He apparently had charge of teaching the educated converts to Christianity in Alexandria. This selection shows his familiarity with classical literature as well as his tendency to ridicule pagan religion while showing somewhat greater sympathy to classical philosophy.

Chapter 1. . . . Inasmuch as the Word was from the first, He was and is the divine source of all things; but inasmuch as He has now assumed the name Christ, consecrated of old, and worthy of power, he has been called by me the New Song. This Word, then, the Christ, the cause of both our being at first (for He was in God) and of our well-being, this very Word has now appeared as man, He alone being both, both God and man—that Author of all blessings to us; by whom we, being taught to live well, are sent on our way to life eternal. For, according to that inspired apostle of the Lord, "the grace of God which bringeth salvation hath appeared to all men, teaching us, that, denying ungodliness and worldly lusts, we should live soberly, righteously, and godly, in this present world; looking for the blessed hope, and appearing of the glory of the great God and our Savior Jesus Christ" [Titus 2:11–13].

This is the New Song, the manifestation of the Word that was in the beginning, and before the beginning. The Savior, who existed before, has in recent days appeared. He, who is in Him that truly is, has appeared; for the Word, who "was with God," and by whom all things were created, has appeared as our Teacher. The Word, who in the beginning bestowed on us life as Creator when He formed us, taught us to live well when He appeared as our Teacher; that as God He might afterwards conduct us to the life which never ends. He did not now for the first time pity us for our error; but He pitied us from the first, from the beginning. But now, at His appearance, lost as we already were, He accomplished our salvation. For that wicked reptile

/

monster, by his enchantments, enslaves and plagues men even till now; inflicting, as seems to me, such barbarous vengeance on them as those who are said to bind the captives to corpses till they rot together. This wicked tyrant and serpent, accordingly, binding fast with the miserable chain of superstition whomsoever he can draw to his side from their birth, to stones, and stocks, and images, and such like idols, may with truth be said to have taken and buried living men with those dead idols, till both suffer corruption together. . . .

Chapter 2. . . . And now, then, hear the loves of your gods,* and the incredible tales of their licentiousness, and their wounds, and their bonds, and their laughings, and their fights, their servitudes too, and their banquets; and furthermore, their embraces, and tears, and sufferings, and lewd delights. Call me Poseidon, and the troop of damsels deflowered by him. Amphitrite, Amymone, Alope, Melanippe, Alcyone, Hippothoe, Chione, and myriads of others; with whom, though so many, the passions of your Poseidon were not satiated. . . .

And, above all, let the father of gods and men, according to you, himself come, who was so given to sexual pleasure, as to lust after all, and indulge his lust on all, like the goats of the Thmuitae. And thy poems, O Homer, fill me with admiration!

> "He said, and nodded with his shadowy brows;
> Waved on the immortal head the ambrosial locks,
> And all Olympus trembled at his nod."
> [*Iliad* 1.528]

Thou makest Zeus venerable, O Homer; and the nod which thou dost ascribe to him is most reverend. But show him only a woman's girdle, and Zeus is exposed, and his locks are dishonored. To what a pitch of licentiousness did that Zeus of yours proceed, who spent so many nights in voluptuousness with Alcmene? For not even these nine nights were long to this insatiable monster. . . .

This is Jupiter the good, the prophetic, the patron of hospitality, the protector of suppliants, the benign, the author of omens, the avenger of wrongs; rather the unjust, the violator of right and of law,

---

*Clement alludes to a whole series of stories, mostly involving the seduction of mortal women by the gods. He concludes with the story of how Zeus transformed himself into a swan in order to seduce Leda.

the impious, the inhuman, the violent, the seducer, the adulterer, the amatory. But perhaps when he was such he was a man; but now these fables seem to have grown old on our hands. Zeus is no longer a serpent, a swan, nor an eagle, nor a licentious man; the god no longer flies, nor loves boys, nor kisses, nor offers violence, although there are still many beautiful women, more comely than Leda, more blooming than Semele, and boys of better looks and manners than the Phrygian herdsman. Where is now that eagle? where now that swan? where now is Zeus himself? He has grown old with his feathers; for as yet he does not repent of his amatory exploits, nor is he taught continence. The fable is exposed before you: Leda is dead, the swan is dead. Seek your Jupiter. Ransack not heaven, but earth. The Cretan, in whose country he was buried, will show him to you,—I mean Callimachus, in his hymns:—

"For thy tomb, O king,
   The Cretans fashioned!"

For Zeus is dead, be not distressed, as Leda is dead, and the swan, and the eagle, and the libertine, and the serpent. And now even the superstitious seem, although reluctantly, yet truly, to have come to understand their error respecting the Gods.

"For not from an ancient oak, nor from a rock,
   But from men is thy descent."
                     [*Odyssey* 19.163]. . . .

Chapter 6. . . . Why, I beseech you, fill up life with idolatrous images, by feigning the winds, or the air, or fire, or earth, or stones, or stocks, or steel, or this universe, to be gods; and, prating loftily of the heavenly bodies in this much vaunted science of astrology, not astronomy, to whom men who have truly wandered, talk of the wandering stars as gods? It is the Lord of the spirits, the Lord of the fire, the Maker of the universe, Him who lighted up the sun, that I long for. I seek after God, not the works of God. Whom shall I take as a helper in my inquiry? We do not, if you have no objection, wholly disown Plato. How, then, is God to be searched out, O Plato? "For both to find the Father and Maker of this universe is a work of difficulty; and having found Him, to declare Him fully, is impossible" [Plato, *Timaeus* 28C].

Why so? by Himself, I beseech you! For He can by no means be expressed. Well done, Plato! Thou hast touched on the truth. . . .

Whence, O Plato, is that hint of the truth which thou givest? Whence this rich copiousness of diction, which proclaims piety with oracular utterance? The tribes of the barbarians, he says, are wiser than these; I know thy teachers, even if thou wouldst conceal them. You have learned geometry from the Egyptians, astronomy from the Babylonians, the charms of healing you have got from the Thracians; the Assyrians also have taught you many things; but for the laws that are consistent with truth, and your sentiments respecting God, you are indebted to the Hebrews.* . . .

Chapter 11. . . . Wherefore, since the Word Himself has come to us from heaven, we need not, I reckon, go any more in search of human learning to Athens and the rest of Greece, and to Ionia. For if we have as our teacher Him that filled the universe with His holy energies in creation, salvation, beneficence, legislation, prophecy, teaching, we have the Teacher from whom all instruction comes; and the whole world, with Athens and Greece, has really become the domain of the Word. For you, who believed the poetical fable which designated Minos the Cretan as the bosom friend of Zeus, will not refuse to believe that we who have become the disciples of God have received the only true wisdom; and that which the chiefs of philosophy only guessed at, the disciples of Christ have both apprehended and proclaimed. And the one whole Christ is not divided: "There is neither barbarian, nor Jew, nor Greek, neither male nor female, but a new man" [Gal. 3:28; 6:15], transformed by God's Holy Spirit.

From *The Ante-Nicene Fathers,* edited and translated by Alexander Roberts and James Donaldson (Buffalo: Christian Literature Company, 1884–1886), Volume 2, pages 173, 179–181, 190–191, 193, 203.

Origen (c.185–c.254)

From *On First Principles*

Origen wrote voluminous biblical commentaries as well as more philosophical analyses of Christianity. In Book 4 of On First Principles *he sets out his methods of biblical interpretation.*

---

*Like a number of other early Christian writers, Clement believed that the Greek poets and philosophers had somehow read the Hebrew Scriptures and had borrowed ideas about God from them.

Book 4

Chapter 1. 8. Having spoken thus briefly on the subject of the divine inspiration of the holy Scriptures, it is necessary to proceed to the (consideration of the) manner in which they are to be read and understood, seeing numerous errors have been committed in consequence of the method in which the holy documents ought to be examined, not having been discovered by the multitude. . . .

9. Now the cause, in all the points previously enumerated, of the false opinions, and of the impious statements or ignorant assertions about God, appears to be nothing else than the not understanding the Scripture according to its spiritual meaning, but the interpretation of it agreeably to the mere letter. . . .

11. The way, then, as it appears to us, in which we ought to deal with the Scriptures, and extract from them their meaning, is the following, which has been ascertained from the Scriptures themselves. By Solomon in the Proverbs we find some such rule as this enjoined respecting the divine doctrines of Scripture: "And do thou portray them in a threefold manner, in counsel and knowledge, to answer words of truth to them who propose them to thee." The individual ought, then, to portray the ideas of holy Scripture in a threefold manner upon his own soul; in order that the simple man may be edified by the "flesh," as it were, of the Scripture, for so we name the obvious sense; while he who has ascended a certain way (may be edified) by the "soul," as it were. The perfect man, again, and he who resembles those spoken of by the apostle, when he says, "We speak wisdom among them that are perfect, but not the wisdom of the world, nor of the rulers of this world, who come to nought; but we speak the wisdom of God in a mystery, the hidden wisdom, which God hath ordained before the ages, unto our glory," (may receive edification) from the spiritual law, which has a shadow of good things to come. For as man consists of body, soul, and spirit, so in the same way does Scripture, which has been arranged to be given by God for the salvation of men. . . .

12. But as there are certain passages of Scripture which do not at all contain the "corporeal" sense, as we shall show in the following (paragraphs), there are also places where we must seek only for the "soul," as it were, and "spirit" of Scripture. And perhaps on this account the water-vessels containing two or three firkins a-piece are said to lie for the purification of the Jews, as we read in the Gospel

according to John:* the expression darkly intimating, with respect to those who (are called) by the apostle "Jews" secretly, that they are purified by the word of Scripture, receiving sometimes two firkins, i.e., so to speak, the "psychical" and "spiritual" sense; and sometimes three firkins, since some have, in addition to those already mentioned, also the "corporeal" sense, which is capable of (producing) edification. And six water-vessels are reasonably (appropriate) to those who are purified in the world, which was made in six days—the perfect number.

That the first "sense," then, is profitable in this respect, that it is capable of imparting edification, is testified by the multitudes of genuine and simple believers; while of that interpretation which is referred back to the "soul," there is an illustration in Paul's first Epistle to the Corinthians. The expression is, "Thou shalt not muzzle the mouth of the ox that treadeth out the corn" [cf. 1 Cor. 9:9–10 and Deut. 25:4]; to which he adds, "Doth God take care of oxen? or saith He it altogether for our sakes? For our sakes, no doubt, this was written: that he that plougheth should plough in hope, and that he who thresheth, in hope of partaking" [cf. 1 Cor. 9:9–10]. And there are numerous interpretations adapted to the multitude which are in circulation, and which edify those who are unable to understand profounder meanings, and which have somewhat the same character.

13. But the interpretation is "spiritual," when one is able to show of what heavenly things the Jews "according to the flesh" served as an example and a shadow, and of what future blessings the law contains a shadow. And, generally, we must investigate, according to the apostolic promise, "the wisdom in a mystery, the hidden wisdom which God ordained before the world for the glory" of the just, which "none of the princes of this world knew" [cf. 1 Cor. 2:6–8]. And the same apostle says somewhere, after referring to certain events mentioned as occurring in Exodus and Numbers, "that these things happened to them figuratively, but that they were written on our account, on whom the ends of the world are come" [1 Cor. 10:11]. And he gives an opportunity for ascertaining of what things these were patterns, when he says: "For they drank of the spiritual Rock that followed them, and that Rock was Christ" [1 Cor. 10:4]. . . .

---

*John 2:6 refers to six water vessels used for Jewish rites of purification, each with a capacity of two or three measures (firkins). Origen finds an allegorical meaning.

And what is most remarkable, by the history of wars, and of the victors, and the vanquished, certain mysteries are indicated to those who are able to test these statements. And more wonderful still, the laws of truth are predicted by the written legislation;—all these being described in a connected series, with a power which is truly in keeping with the wisdom of God. For it was intended that the covering also of the spiritual truths—I mean the "bodily" part of Scripture—should not be without profit in many cases, but should be capable of improving the multitude, according to their capacity. . . .

16. For who that has understanding will suppose that the first, and second, and third day, and the evening and the morning, existed without a sun, and moon, and stars? and the first day was, as it were, also without a sky? And who is so foolish as to suppose that God, after the manner of a husbandman, planted a paradise in Eden, towards the east, and placed in it a tree of life, visible and palpable, so that one tasting of the fruit by the bodily teeth obtained life? and again, that one was a partaker of good and evil by masticating what was taken from the tree? And if God is said to walk in the paradise in the evening, and Adam to hide himself under a tree, I do not suppose that any one doubts that these things figuratively indicate certain mysteries, the history having taken place in appearance, and not literally.

Cain also, when going forth from the presence of God, certainly appears to thoughtful men as likely to lead the reader to inquire what is the presence of God, and what is the meaning of going out from Him. And what need is there to say more, since those who are not altogether blind can collect countless instances of a similar kind recorded as having occurred, but which did not literally take place?

Nay, the Gospels themselves are filled with the same kind of narratives; e.g., the devil leading Jesus up into a high mountain, in order to show him from thence the kingdoms of the whole world, and the glory of them. For who is there among those who do not read such accounts carelessly, that would not condemn those who think that with the eye of the body—which requires a lofty height in order that the parts lying (immediately) under and adjacent may be seen— the kingdoms of the Persians, and Scythians, and Indians, and Parthians, were beheld, and the manner in which their princes are glorified among men? And the attentive reader may notice in the Gospels innumerable other passages like these, so that he will be convinced that in the histories that are literally recorded, circumstances that did not occur are inserted. . . .

18. All these statements have been made by us, in order to show that the design of that divine power which gave us the Scriptures is, that we should not receive what is presented by the letter alone (such things being sometimes not true in their literal acceptation, but absurd and impossible), but that certain things have been introduced into the actual history and into the legislation that are useful in their literal sense.

19. But that no one may suppose that we assert respecting the whole that no history is real because a certain one is not; and that no law is to be literally observed, because a certain one, (understood) according to the letter, is absurd or impossible; or that the statements regarding the Saviour are not true in a manner perceptible to the senses; or that no commandment and precept of His ought to be obeyed;—we have to answer that, with regard to certain things, it is perfectly clear to us that the historical account is true; as that Abraham was buried in the double cave at Hebron, as also Isaac and Jacob, and the wives of each of them; and that Shechem was given as a portion to Joseph [cf. Gen. 48:22 and Josh. 24:32]; and that Jerusalem is the metropolis of Judea, in which the temple of God was built by Solomon; and innumerable other statements. For the passages that are true in their historical meaning are much more numerous than those which are interspersed with a purely spiritual signification.

In the fourth century, Rufinus translated Origen's On First Principles *into Latin. The translation was a free one, in which Rufinus elaborated and explained some of Origen's points, but parts of the text, such as the selection that follows, survived only in the Latin version. The emphasis on human free will and the hope of universal salvation presented in this selection certainly come from Origen, but the wording may often not be his.*

Book 1

Chapter 6. 1. . . . The end of the world, then, and the final consummation, will take place when every one shall be subjected to punishment for his sins; a time which God alone knows, when He will bestow on each one what he deserves. We think, indeed, that the goodness of God, through His Christ, may recall all His creatures to one end, even His enemies being conquered and subdued. For thus says holy Scripture, "The Lord said to My Lord, Sit Thou at My right hand, until I make Thine enemies Thy footstool" [Ps. 110:1]. And if the meaning of the prophet's language here be less clear, we may ascertain it from the Apostle Paul, who speaks more openly thus: "For Christ must reign until He has put all enemies under His feet" [1 Cor. 15:25]. But if even that unreserved declaration of the apostle do not sufficiently inform us what is meant by "enemies being placed under His feet," listen to what he says in the following words, "For all things must be put under Him." What, then, is this "putting under" by which all things must be made subject to Christ? I am of opinion that it is this very subjection by which we also wish to be subject to Him, by which the apostles also were subject, and all the saints who have been followers of Christ. For the name "subjection," by which we are subject to Christ, indicates that the salvation which proceeds from Him belongs to His subjects, agreeably to the declaration of David, "Shall not my soul be subject unto God? From Him cometh my salvation" [Ps. 62:1].

2. Seeing, then, that such is the end, when all enemies will be subdued to Christ, when death—the last enemy—shall be destroyed, and when the kingdom shall be delivered up by Christ (to whom all things are subject) to God the Father; let us, I say, from such an end as this, contemplate the beginnings of things. For the end is always like the beginning: and, therefore, as there is one end to all things, so ought we to understand that there was one beginning; and as there is one end to many things, so there spring from one beginning many differences and varieties, which again, through the goodness of God, and by subjection to Christ, and through the unity of the Holy Spirit, are recalled to one end, which is like unto the beginning: all those, viz., who, bending the knee at the name of Jesus, make known by so doing their subjection to Him: and these are they who are in heaven, on earth, and under the earth: by which three classes the whole universe of things is pointed out, those, viz., who from that one beginning were arranged, each according to the diversity of his conduct, among the different orders, in accordance with their desert; for there was no goodness in them by essential being, as in God and His Christ, and in the Holy Spirit. For in the Trinity alone, which is the author of all things, does goodness exist in virtue of essential being; while others possess it as an accidental and perishable quality, and only then enjoy blessedness, when they participate in holiness and wisdom, and in divinity itself.

But if they neglect and despise such participation, then is each one, by fault of his own slothfulness, made, one more rapidly, another more slowly, one in a greater, another in a less degree, the cause of his own downfall. And since, as we have remarked, the lapse by which an individual falls away from his position is characterized by great diversity, according to the movements of the mind and will, one man falling with greater ease, another with more difficulty, into a lower condition; in this is to be seen the just judgment of the providence of God, that it should happen to every one according to the diversity of his conduct, in proportion to the desert of his declension and defection. . . .

But those who have been removed from their primal state of blessedness have not been removed irrecoverably, but have been placed under the rule of those holy and blessed orders* which we have described; and by availing themselves of the aid of these, and being remoulded by salutary principles and discipline, they may recover themselves, and be restored to their condition of happiness. From all which I am of opinion, so far as I can see, that this order of the human race has been appointed in order that in the future world, or in ages to come, when there shall be the new heavens and new earth, spoken of by Isaiah, it may be restored to that unity promised by the Lord Jesus in His prayer to God the Father on behalf of His disciples: "I do not pray for these alone, but for all who shall believe on Me through their word: that they all may be one, as Thou, Father, art in Me, and I in Thee, that they also may be one in Us" [John 17:20, 21]. . . .

But in the meantime, both in those temporal worlds which are seen, as well as in those eternal worlds which are invisible, all those beings are arranged, according to a regular plan, in the order and degree of their merits; so that some of them in the first, others in the second, some even in the last times, after having undergone heavier and severer punishments, endured for a lengthened period, and for many ages, so to speak, improved by this stern method of training, and restored at first by the instruction of the angels, and subsequently by the powers of a higher grade, and thus advancing through each stage to a better condition, reach even to that which is invisible and eternal, having travelled through, by a kind of training, every single office of the heavenly powers. From which, I think, this will appear to follow as an inference, that every rational nature may, in passing from one order to another, go through each to all, and advance from

---

*The angels.

all to each, while made the subject of various degrees of proficiency and failure according to its own actions and endeavours, put forth in the enjoyment of its power of freedom of will.

Translated by Frederick Crombie. From *The Ante-Nicene Fathers,* edited by Alexander Roberts and James Donaldson (Buffalo: Christian Literature Company, 1884–1886), Volume 4, pages 355–357, 359–361, 363, 365–368, 260–261.

Tertullian (c.150–c.220)

From *On Prescription Against Heretics*

Tertullian lived in what is now Tunisia. He wrote an Apology and a range of attacks against heretics. In this first selection, having summarized the mistaken ideas of the heretics, he turns to argue that those mistakes grow out of their dependence on philosophy.

Chapter 7. These are "the doctrines" of men and "of demons" [1 Tim. 4:1] produced for itching ears of the spirit of this world's wisdom: this the Lord called "foolishness" [1 Cor. 3:18, 25], and "chose the foolish things of the world" to confound even philosophy itself. For (philosophy) it is which is the material of the world's wisdom, the rash interpreter of the nature and the dispensation of God. Indeed heresies are themselves instigated by philosophy. From this source came the Aeons, and I know not what infinite forms, and the trinity of man in the system of Valentinus, who was of Plato's school. From the same source came Marcion's better god, with all his tranquillity; he came of the Stoics. Then, again, the opinion that the soul dies is held by the Epicureans; while the denial of the restoration of the body is taken from the aggregate school of all the philosophers; also, when matter is made equal to God, then you have the teaching of Zeno; and when any doctrine is alleged touching a god of fire, then Heraclitus comes in.* The same subject-matter is discussed over and over again by the heretics and the philosophers; the same arguments are involved. Whence comes evil? Why is it permitted? What is the origin of man? and in what way does he come? . . . Unhappy Aristotle! who invented for these men dialectics,

---

*Valentinus was a Gnostic teacher. The Epicureans were a school of Greek philosophers. Zeno of Citium (c.336–c.265 B.C.) founded Stoicism. Heraclitus of Ephesus, who lived around 500 B.C., wrote, "There is an exchange of all things for fire, and of fire for all things."

the art of building up and pulling down; an art so evasive in its propositions, so farfetched in its conjectures, so harsh in its arguments, so productive of contentions—embarrassing even to itself, retracting everything, and really treating of nothing! Whence spring those "fables and endless genealogies" [1 Tim. 1:4], and "unprofitable questions" [Titus 3:9], and "words which spread like a cancer"? [2 Tim. 2:17]. From all these, when the apostle would restrain us, he expressly names *philosophy* as that which he would have us be on our guard against. Writing to the Colossians, he says, "See that no one beguile you through philosophy and vain deceit, after the tradition of men, and contrary to the wisdom of the Holy Ghost" [Col. 2:8]. He had been at Athens, and had in his interviews (with its philosophers) become acquainted with that human wisdom which pretends to know the truth, whilst it only corrupts it, and is itself divided into its own manifold heresies, by the variety of its mutually repugnant sects. What indeed has Athens to do with Jerusalem? What concord is there between the Academy and the Church? what between heretics and Christians? Our instruction comes from "the porch of Solomon,"* who had himself taught that "the Lord should be sought in simplicity of heart" [Wisd. of Sol. 1:1]. Away with all attempts to produce a mottled Christianity of Stoic, Platonic, and dialectic composition! We want no curious disputation after possessing Christ Jesus, no inquisition after enjoying the gospel! With our faith, we desire no further belief. For this is our palmary faith, that there is nothing which we ought to believe besides.

Translated by Peter Holmes. From *The Ante-Nicene Fathers,* edited by Alexander Roberts and James Donaldson (Buffalo: Christian Literature Company, 1884–1886), Volume 3, page 246.

Tertullian

From *Apology*

For all Tertullian's denunciations of philosophy, as this selection shows, he knew the works of Stoic philosophers such as Zeno and

---

*The Stoics were often known as the school of "the porch" because their founder, Zeno, had taught in the porch of a temple in Athens. Acts 3:5 describes how the apostles taught in Solomon's porch in the Temple of Jerusalem.

Cleanthes (c.331–232 B.C.) and could use their ideas, as well as a range of images, to explain what he believed about Christ. Cleanthes' famous "Hymn to Zeus" represents one of the purest statements of monotheism in pagan literature.

Chapter 21. . . . We have already asserted that God made the world, and all which it contains, by His Word, and Reason, and Power. It is abundantly plain that your philosophers, too, regard the Logos—that is, the Word and Reason—as the Creator of the universe. For Zeno lays it down that he is the creator, having made all things according to a determinate plan; that his name is Fate, and God, and the soul of Jupiter, and the necessity of all things. Cleanthes ascribes all this to spirit, which he maintains pervades the universe. And we, in like manner, hold that the Word, and Reason, and Power, by which we have said God made all, have spirit as their proper and essential *substratum,* in which the Word has inbeing to give forth utterances, and reason abides to dispose and arrange, and power is over all to execute. We have been taught that He proceeds forth from God, and in that procession He is generated; so that He is the Son of God, and is called God from unity of substance with God. For God, too, is a Spirit. Even when the ray is shot from the sun, it is still part of the parent mass; the sun will still be in the ray, because it is a ray of the sun—there is no division of substance, but merely an extension. Thus Christ is Spirit of Spirit, and God of God, as light of light is kindled. The material matrix remains entire and unimpaired, though you derive from it any number of shoots possessed of its qualities; so, too, that which has come forth out of God is at once God and the Son of God, and the two are one. In this way also, as He is Spirit of Spirit and God of God, He is made a second in manner of existence—in position, not in nature; and He did not withdraw from the original source, but went forth. This ray of God, then, as it was always foretold in ancient times, descending into a certain virgin, and made flesh in her womb, is in His birth God and man united. The flesh formed by the Spirit is nourished, grows up to manhood, speaks, teaches, works, and is the Christ.

Translated by S. Thelwell. From *The Ante-Nicene Fathers,* edited by Alexander Roberts and James Donaldson (Buffalo: Christian Literature Company, 1884–1886), Volume 3, pages 34–35.

Tertullian

From *On the Flesh of Christ*

Tertullian wrote this treatise to criticize Marcion's claim that Christ had not had a true human body. The chapter just before this selection insists on the human reality of Christ's birth in the face of Marcion's discomfort at associating the divinity with the physical details of a human birth.

Chapter 5. There are, to be sure, other things also quite as foolish (as the birth of Christ), which have reference to the humiliations and sufferings of God. Or else, let them call a crucified God "wisdom." But Marcion will apply the knife to this *doctrine* also, and even with greater reason. For which is more unworthy of God, which is more likely to raise a blush of shame, that *God* should be born, or that He should die? that He should bear the flesh, or the cross? be circumcised, or be crucified? be cradled, or be coffined? be laid in a manger, or in a tomb? *Talk of "wisdom"!* You will show more of *that* if you refuse to believe this also. But, after all, you will not be "wise" unless you become a "fool" to the world, by believing "the foolish things of God." Have you, then, cut away all sufferings from Christ, on the ground that, as a mere phantom, He was incapable of experiencing them? We have said above that He might possibly have undergone the unreal mockeries of an imaginary birth and infancy. But answer me at once, you that murder truth: Was not God really crucified? And, having been really crucified, did He not really die? And, having indeed really died, did He not really rise again? Falsely did Paul "determine to know nothing amongst us but Jesus and him crucified" [1 Cor. 2:2]; falsely has he impressed upon us that He was buried; falsely inculcated that He rose again. False, therefore, is our faith also. And all that we hope for from Christ will be a phantom. O thou most infamous of men, who acquittest of all guilt the murderers of God! For nothing did Christ suffer from them, if He really suffered nothing at all. Spare the whole world's one only hope, thou who art destroying the indispensable dishonor of our faith. Whatsoever is unworthy of God, is of gain to me. I am safe, if I am not ashamed of my Lord. "Whosoever," says He, "shall be ashamed of me, of him will I also be ashamed" [Matt. 10:33; Mark 8:38; Luke 9:26]. Other matters for shame find I none which can prove me to be shameless in a good sense, and foolish in a happy one, by my own contempt of shame. The Son of God was crucified; I am not ashamed because men must needs be ashamed *of it.* And the Son of God died; it is by all means to be believed, because it is absurd. And He was buried and rose again; the fact is certain, because it is impossible. But how will all this be true in Him, if He was not Himself true—if He really had not in himself that which might be crucified, might die, might be buried, and might rise again?

Translated by Peter Holmes. From *The Ante-Nicene Fathers,* edited by Alexander Roberts and James Donaldson (Buffalo: Christian Literature Company, 1884–1886), Volume 3, pages 525–526.

CHAPTER 3

The Trinitarian
and Christological Controversies

Jesus' first disciples knew him as a human being who walked with them, and thirsted, and wept. As Jews, they believed in one God. Yet Christians soon came to pray to Jesus Christ, to worship him, to rely on him for their salvation. All that made sense only if Christ were God. But how could a human being be God? And if Christ was God, how could there be only one God?

In the struggle against Gnosticism, most Christians rejected Docetism—the idea that Christ had only *appeared* to be human—and accepted his full humanity. In Rome about 200 Sabellius and others asserted that Christ was simply identical with God. But that seemed too simple, and not quite right. After all, Christ prayed to "the Father," and many passages in the New Testament distinguished between "Father" and "Son."

In the early 300s, in Alexandria in Egypt, Arius tried to clarify these issues and, in doing so, split the Christian community. Christ, he said, is divine, but not actually God—a lesser kind of divinity. The Son was not eternal but came into being when the Father "begot" him; "there was a time when he was not." Arius' great opponent Athanasius argued that the Son *was* eternal, and of the *same* substance *(homoousios)*, not merely of *similar* substance *(homoiousios)* with the Father. The Emperor Constantine, newly converted to Christianity, found this Arian dispute dividing his Christian subjects. He called a council at Nicaea in 325, where Athanasius and the forces of *homoousios* carried the day.

But that left many questions unanswered. Christians had long baptized "in the name of the Father and the Son and the Holy Ghost," so it seemed that the Holy Spirit ought to share in whatever one said about the Father and the Son. Somehow, then, God was one but also three. Two brothers and a good friend of theirs, all from Cappadocia, in what is now Turkey—Basil, Gregory of Nyssa, and Gregory of Nazianzus—developed clarifying terminology. God, they said, was a Trinity: one *ousia* or essence, but three *hypostases* or particular individuals. Christians who spoke Latin came to refer to one *substantia* and three *personae.*

To the extent one could, that clarified the relation of Father and Son (and Holy Spirit). But what about the relation of human and divine in Christ? The Alexandrian tradition had always talked about the Divine Word and the human flesh. In the late 300s an Alexandrian Christian named Apollinaris tried to make the implications of this view clearer. Christ, he said, had a human body but not a human mind; the divine *Logos* took the place of such a mind. To his critics, Apollinaris seemed to be denying Christ's full humanity. A theological tradition centered on Antioch in Syria and represented by Theodore of Mopsuestia had come to speak of Christ's "two natures," human and divine. That preserved Christ's full humanity, but Nestorius, preaching in Constantinople in the early 400s, got into trouble by pursuing this "two-natures" Christology to an extreme. Many Christians had begun to pray to Mary as *"theotokos,"* the bearer or Mother of God. Nestorius insisted this was wrong, for Mary was only mother of the human nature. Cyril of Alexandria denounced Nestorius, proclaiming that after the Incarnation Christ had only "one nature" and steamrolling his views to victory at the Council of Ephesus in 431. Even some other opponents of Nestorius thought Cyril had gone too far. In 451 the Council of Chalcedon declared that even after the Incarnation there were two natures, but they were so united in one person that the predicates of one could be applied to the other, and thus, among other things, one could indeed call Mary the Mother of God. "Monophysite" (from *monophysis,* one nature) Christians still survive in the Coptic Church of Egypt, and "Nestorian" Christians spread throughout much of Asia, but the Chalcedonian compromise set the terms of orthodoxy for most Christians.

Athanasius (c.298–373)

From *On the Incarnation of the Word*

Athanasius attended the Council of Nicaea in 325 as a young deacon and spent the rest of his long life—after 328 he was bishop of Alexandria—defending its conclusions. That defense involved him in risk of death, arguments with the emperor, and five exiles. He wrote On the Incarnation of the Word *as a young man, before the Arian controversy erupted; it states the fundamental principles of his theology in nonpolemical fashion.*

6. . . . Death having gained upon men, and corruption abiding upon them, the race of man was perishing; the rational man made

in God's image was disappearing, and the handiwork of God was in process of dissolution. For death, as I said above, gained from that time forth a legal hold over us, and it was impossible to evade the law, since it had been laid down by God because of the transgression, and the result was in truth at once monstrous and unseemly. For it were monstrous, firstly, that God, having spoken, should prove false—that, when once He had ordained that man, if he transgressed the commandment, should die the death, after the transgression man should not die, but God's word should be broken. For God would not be true, if, when He had said we should die, man died not. Again, it were unseemly that creatures once made rational, and having partaken of the Word, should go to ruin, and turn again toward non-existence by the way of corruption. For it were not worthy of God's goodness that the things He had made should waste away, because of the deceit practiced on men by the devil. Especially it was unseemly to the last degree that God's handicraft among men should be done away, either because of their own carelessness, or because of the deceitfulness of evil spirits. So, as the rational creatures were wasting and such works in course of ruin, what was God in His goodness to do? Suffer corruption to prevail against them and death to hold them fast? And where were the profit of their having been made, to begin with? For better were they not made, than once made, left to neglect and ruin. . . .

8. For this purpose, then, the incorporeal and incorruptible and immaterial Word of God comes to our realm, howbeit he was not far from us before [Acts 17:27]. For no part of Creation is left void of Him: He has filled all things everywhere, remaining present with His own Father. But He comes in condescension to shew loving-kindness upon us, and to visit us. . . .

He takes unto Himself a body, and that of no different sort from ours. For He did not simply will to become embodied, or will merely to appear. For if He willed merely to appear, He was able to effect His divine appearance by some other and higher means as well. But He takes a body of our kind, and not merely so, but from a spotless and stainless virgin, knowing not a man, a body clean and in very truth pure from intercourse of men. For being Himself mighty, and Artificer of everything, He prepares the body in the Virgin as a temple unto Himself, and makes it His very own as an instrument, in it manifested, and in it dwelling. And thus taking from our bodies one of like nature, because all were under penalty of the corruption of death He gave it over to death in the stead of all, and offered it to the Father—doing this, moreover, of His loving-kindness, to the end that, firstly, all being held to have died in Him, the law involving the ruin of men might be undone (inasmuch as its power was fully spent in the Lord's body, and had no longer holding-ground against men, his peers), and that, secondly, whereas men had turned toward corruption, He might turn them again toward incorruption, and quicken them from death by the appropriation of His body and by the grace of the Resurrection, banishing death from them like straw from the fire. . . .

9. . . . And thus He, the incorruptible Son of God, being conjoined with all by a like nature, naturally clothed all with incorruption, by the promise of the resurrection. For the actual corruption in death has no longer holding-ground against men, by reason of the Word, which by His one body has come to dwell among them. And like as when a great king has entered into some large city and taken up his abode in one of the houses there, such city is at all events held worthy of high honor, nor does any enemy or bandit any longer descend upon it and subject it; but, on the contrary, it is thought entitled to all care, because of the king's having taken up his residence in a single house there: so, too, has it been with the Monarch of all. For now that He has come to our realm, and taken up his abode in one body among His peers, henceforth the whole conspiracy of the enemy against mankind is checked, and the corruption of death which before was prevailing against them is done away. For the race of men had gone to ruin, had not the Lord and Saviour of all, the Son of God, come among us to meet the end of death.

Translated by Archibald Robertson. From *Nicene and Post-Nicene Fathers,* 2nd Series, edited by Philip Schaff and Henry Wace (New York: Christian Literature Company, 1890–1900), Volume 4, pages 39–41.

Arius (c.250–336)

From *Letter to Eusebius of Nicomedia*

Arius, a deacon in the church of Alexandria, defended his theological views in every way, even writing popular songs setting out his position. Under the guidance of Athanasius, Alexander, the Bishop or Patriarch of Alexandria—the title "Pope" was also applied to the

*bishop of Alexandria—had attacked Arius, who is here writing to a
bishop he hopes will share his views, protesting the persecution he has
suffered.*

To his very dear lord, the man of God, the faithful and orthodox
Eusebius, Arius, unjustly persecuted by Alexander the Pope, on
account of that all-conquering truth of which you also are a cham-
pion, sendeth greeting in the Lord. . . .

The bishop greatly wastes and persecutes us, and leaves no stone
unturned against us. He has driven us out of the city as atheists,
because we do not concur in what he publicly preaches, namely God
always, the Son always; as the Father so the Son; the Son co-exists
unbegotten with God; He is everlasting; neither by thought nor by
any interval does God precede the Son; always God, always Son; he
is begotten of the unbegotten; the Son is of God Himself. . . .

But we say and believe, and have taught, and do teach, that the
Son is not unbegotten, nor in any way part of the unbegotten; and
that He does not derive His subsistence from any matter; but that
by His own will and counsel He has subsisted before time, and before
ages, as perfect God, only begotten and unchangeable, and that
before He was begotten, or created, or purposed, or established, He
was not. For He was not unbegotten. We are persecuted, because we
say that the Son has a beginning, but that God is without beginning.
This is the cause of our persecution, and likewise, because we say that
He is of the non-existent. And this we say, because He is neither part
of God, nor of any essential being.

Translated by Blomfield Jackson. From *Nicene and Post-Nicene Fathers,* 2nd Series,
edited by Philip Schaff and Henry Wace (New York: Christian Literature Company,
1890–1900), Volume 3, page 41.

The Nicene Creed

*Written at the first great council of the church, a gathering of
bishops called by the Emperor Constantine which met in 325, this
creed rejected the views of the Arians, though debates about how to
interpret it broke out as soon as the council adjourned. The "Nicene
Creed" used in Christian worship today is usually a slightly modified
version of a revision written at the Second Council of Constantinople
in 381; what follows is a translation of the original text adopted at
Nicaea.*

We believe in one God, the Father Almighty, maker of all things, visible and invisible; and in one Lord Jesus Christ, the Son of God, the only-begotten of his Father, of the substance of the Father, God of God, Light of Light, very God of very God, begotten, not made, being of one substance with the Father. By whom all things were made, both which be in heaven and in earth. Who for us men and for our salvation came down [from heaven] and was incarnate and was made man. He suffered and the third day he rose again, and ascended into heaven. And he shall come again to judge both the quick and the dead. And [we believe] in the Holy Ghost. And whosoever shall say that there was a time when the Son of God was not, or that before he was begotten he was not, or that he was made of things that were not, or that he is of a different substance or essence [from the Father] or that he is a creature, or subject to change or conversion—all that so say, the Catholic and Apostolic Church anathematizes them.

Translated by Henry R. Percival. From *Nicene and Post-Nicene Fathers,* 2nd Series, edited by Philip Schaff and Henry Wace (New York: Christian Literature Company, 1890–1900), Volume 14, page 3.

Athanasius

From *First Discourse Against the Arians*

Athanasius wrote these orations from exile in the deserts of Egypt, defending the Nicene Creed in the face of the renewed Arian forces, who won imperial support in the years after the Council of Nicaea. He mentions the Thalia, a book in which Arius had set out his views.

Chapter 1. 1. Of all the other heresies which have departed from the truth it is acknowledged that they have but devised a madness, and their irreligiousness has long since become notorious to all men. . . . But, whereas one heresy, and that the last, which has now risen as harbinger of Antichrist, the Arian, as it is called, considering that other heresies, her elder sisters, have been openly proscribed, in her craft and cunning, affects to array herself in Scripture language, like her father the devil, and is forcing her way back into the Church's paradise. . . . I have thought it necessary, at your request, to unrip "the folds of its breast-plate," and to shew the ill savour of its folly. . . .

Chapter 2. 5. . . . And the mockeries which he [Arius] utters in it, repulsive and most irreligious, are such as these: "God was not always a Father"; but "once God was alone, and not yet a Father, but afterwards He became a Father." "The Son was not always," for, whereas all things were made out of nothing, and all existing creatures and works were made, so the Word of God Himself was "made out of nothing," and "once He was not," and "He was not before His origination," but He as others "had an origin of creation." "For God," he says, "was alone, and the Word as yet was not, nor the Wisdom. Then, wishing to form us, thereupon He made a certain one, and named Him Word and Wisdom and Son, that He might form us by means of Him." . . .

6. Moreover he has dared to say, that "the Word is not the very God"; "though He is called God, yet He is not very God," but "by participation of grace, He, as others, is God only in name." And, whereas all beings are foreign and different from God in essence, so too is "the Word alien and unlike in all things to the Father's essence and propriety," but belongs to things originated and created, and is one of these. Afterwards, as though he had succeeded to the devil's recklessness, he has stated in his *Thalia,* that "even to the Son the Father is invisible," and "the Word cannot perfectly and exactly either see or know His own Father"; but even what He knows and what He sees, He knows and sees "in proportion to His own measure," as we also know according to our own power. For the Son, too, he says, not only knows not the Father exactly, for He fails in comprehension, but "He knows not even His own essence"; and that "the essences of the Father and the Son and the Holy Ghost, are separate in nature, and estranged, and disconnected, and alien, and without participation of each other"; and, in his own words, "utterly unlike from each other in essence and glory, unto infinity." Thus as to "likeness or glory and essence," he says that the Word is entirely diverse from both the Father and the Holy Ghost. . . .

9. For, behold, we take divine Scripture, and thence discourse with freedom of the religious Faith, and set it up as a light upon its candlestick, saying: Very Son of the Father, natural and genuine, proper to His essence, Wisdom Only-begotten, and Very and Only Word of God is He; not a creature or work, but an offspring proper to the Father's essence. Wherefore He is very God, existing one in essence [*homoousios*] with the very Father; while other beings, to whom He said, "I said ye are Gods" [Ps. 82:6], had this grace from the Father, only by participation of the Word, through the Spirit.

For He is the expression of the Father's Person, and Light from Light, and Power, and very Image of the Father's essence. For this too the Lord has said, "He that hath seen me, hath seen the Father" [John 14:9]. And He ever was and is, and never was not. For the Father being everlasting, His Word and His Wisdom must be ever-lasting. . . .

10. Which of the two theologies sets forth our Lord Jesus Christ as God and Son of the Father, this which you vomited forth, or that which we have spoken and maintain from the Scriptures? If the Saviour be not God, nor Word, nor Son, you shall have leave to say what you will, and so shall the Gentiles, and the present Jews. But if He be Word of the Father and true Son, and God from God, and "over all blessed for ever" [Rom. 9:5], is it not becoming to obliterate and blot out those other phrases and that Arian *Thalia* as but a pattern of evil, a store of all irreligion, into which, whoso falls, "knoweth not that giants perish with her, and reacheth the depths of Hades?" [Prov. 9:18, Septuagint]. . . .

For who is there in all mankind, Greek or Barbarian, who ventures to rank among creatures One whom he confesses the while to be God, and says, that He was not till He was made? or who is there, who to the God in whom he has put faith, refuses to give credit, when He says, "This is My beloved Son" [Matt. 3:17], on the pretence that He is not a Son, but a creature? rather such madness would rouse an universal indignation.

Translated by Archibald Robertson. From *Nicene and Post-Nicene Fathers,* 2nd Series, edited by Philip Schaff and Henry Wace (New York: Christian Literature Company, 1890–1900), Volume 4, pages 306, 308–309, 311–312.

Basil of Caesarea (c.329–379)

From *Letters*

Basil was a figure of towering importance, a skilled politician, a theologian, and the organizer of much of the tradition of Greek monasticism. These passages come from three of his letters, the first to the "canonicae," a group of women specially devoted to church work and prayer.

Letter 52. To the Canonicae
1. . . . In us both there is one mind about the faith, as being heirs of the same Fathers who once at Nicaea promulgated their great

decree concerning the faith. Of this, some portions are universally accepted without cavil, but the term *homoousion,* ill received in certain quarters, is still rejected by some. . . .

2. Because even at that time there were men who asserted the Son to have been brought into being out of the non-existent, the term *homoousion* was adopted, to extirpate this impiety. For the conjunction of the Son with the Father is without time and without interval. The preceding words show this to have been the intended meaning. For after saying that the Son was light of light, and begotten of the substance of the Father, but was not made, they went on to add the *homoousion,* thereby showing that whatever proportion of light any one would attribute in the case of the Father will obtain also in that of the Son. For very light in relation to very light, according to the actual sense of light, will have no variation. . . .

3. This term also corrects the error of Sabellius,* for it removes the idea of the identity of the *hypostases,* and introduces in perfection the idea of the Persons. For nothing can be of one substance with itself, but one thing is of one substance with another. The word has therefore an excellent and orthodox use, defining as it does both the proper character of the *hypostases,* and setting forth the invariability of the nature. And when we are taught that the Son is of the substance of the Father, begotten and not made, let us not fall into the material sense of the relations. For the substance was not separated from the Father and bestowed on the Son; neither did the substance engender by fluxion, nor yet by shooting forth as plants their fruits. The mode of the divine begetting is ineffable and inconceivable by human thought.

Letter 159. To Eupaterius and his daughter

2. But since the question now raised by those who are always endeavoring to introduce novelties, but passed over in silence by the men of old, because the doctrine was never gainsaid, has remained without full explanation (I mean that which concerns the Holy Ghost) I will add a statement on this subject in conformity with the sense of Scripture. As we were baptized, so we profess our belief. As we profess our belief, so also we offer praise. As then baptism has been given us by the Saviour, in the name of the Father and of the Son and

---

*The actual views of Sabellius, who taught in Rome in the third century, remain uncertain, but he was later comdemned for teaching that the one God revealed himself in three different ways (Creator, Redeemer, Sanctifier) but was not really three distinct persons.

of the Holy Ghost, so, in accordance with our baptism, we make the confession of the creed, and our doxology in accordance with our creed. We glorify the Holy Ghost together with the Father and the Son, from the conviction that He is not separated from the Divine Nature; for that which is foreign by nature does not share in the same honors. All who call the Holy Ghost a creature we pity, on the ground that, by this utterance, they are falling into the unpardonable sin of blasphemy against Him. I need use no argument to prove to those who are even slightly trained in Scripture, that the creature is separated from the Godhead. The creature is a slave; but the Spirit sets free [Rom. 8:2]. The creature needs life; the Spirit is the Giver of life [John 6:63]. The creature requires teaching. It is the Spirit that teaches [John 14:26]. The creature is sanctified; it is the Spirit that sanctifies [Rom. 15:16]. Whether you name angels, archangels, or all the heavenly powers, they receive their sanctification through the Spirit, but the Spirit Himself has His holiness by nature, not received by favor, but essentially His; whence He has received the distinctive name of Holy. What then is by nature holy, as the Father is by nature holy, and the Son by nature holy, we do not ourselves allow to be separated and severed from the divine and blessed Trinity, nor accept those who rashly reckon it as part of creation.

Letter 236. To Amphilochius

6. The distinction between *ousia* and *hypostasis* is the same as that between the general and the particular; as, for instance, between the animal and the particular man. Wherefore, in the case of the Godhead, we confess one essence or substance so as not to give a variant definition of existence, but we confess a particular *hypostasis,* in order that our conception of Father, Son and Holy Spirit may be without confusion and clear. If we have no distinct perception of the separate characteristics, namely, fatherhood, sonship, and sanctification, but form our conception of God from the general idea of existence, we cannot possibly give a sound account of our faith. We must, therefore, confess the faith by adding the particular to the common. The Godhead is common; the fatherhood particular. We must therefore combine the two and say, "I believe in God the Father." The like course must be pursued in the confession of the Son; we must combine the particular with the common and say "I believe in God the Son," so in the case of the Holy Ghost we must make our utterance conform to the appellation and say "in God the Holy Ghost." Hence it results that there is a satisfactory preservation

of the unity by the confession of the one Godhead, while in the distinction of the individual properties regarded in each there is the confession of the peculiar properties of the Persons.

Translated by Blomfield Jackson. From *Nicene and Post-Nicene Fathers,* 2nd Series, edited by Philip Schaff and Henry Wace (New York: Christian Literature Company, 1890–1900), Volume 8, pages 155–156, 212, 278.

Gregory of Nazianzus (c.330–c.390)

From *The Third Theological Oration*

Basil's friend Gregory of Nazianzus had a troubled and often unhappy career, but at a crucial moment in 379 he became archbishop of Constantinople. The imperial capital had had a series of Arian archbishops, but Gregory now defended the Nicene Creed and the Trinity in a series of theological orations. At the beginning of this selection he addresses the question of why only the first Person of the Trinity is described as "without origin" or "unoriginate," since all three persons are eternal.

2. . . . This is what we mean by Father and Son and Holy Ghost. The Father is the Begetter and the Emitter; without passion of course, and without reference to time, and not in a corporeal manner. The Son is the Begotten, and the Holy Ghost the Emission; for I know not how this could be expressed in terms altogether excluding visible things. . . .

3. When did these come into being? They are above all "When." But, if I am to speak with something more of boldness,—when the Father did. And when did the Father come into being? There never was a time when He was not. And the same thing is true of the Son and the Holy Ghost. . . .

How then are They not alike unoriginate, if They are coeternal? Because They are from Him, though not after Him. For that which is unoriginate is eternal, but that which is eternal is not necessarily unoriginate, so long as it may be referred to the Father as its origin. Therefore in respect to Cause They are not unoriginate; but it is evident that the Cause is not necessarily prior to its effects, for the sun is not prior to its light. . . .

But, the objector says, the very form of the expression "He begat" and "He was begotten" brings in the idea of a beginning of generation. But what if you do not use this expression, but say, "He had been begotten from the beginning" so as readily to evade your far-fetched and time-loving objections? . . .

8. How then was He begotten? This Generation would have been no great thing, if you could have comprehended it who have no real knowledge even of your own generation, or at least who comprehend very little of it, and of that little you are ashamed to speak; and then do you think you know the whole? You will have to undergo much labor before you discover the laws of composition, formation, manifestation, and the bond whereby soul is united to body,—mind to soul, and reason to mind. . . . Tell me what these laws are? And do not even then venture to speculate on the Generation of God; for that would be unsafe. For even if you knew all about your own, yet you do not by any means know about God's. . . . The Begetting of God must be honored by silence. It is a great thing for you to learn that He was begotten. But the manner of His generation we will not admit that even Angels can conceive, much less you. Shall I tell you how it was? It was in a manner known to the Father Who begat, and to the Son Who was begotten. Any more than this is hidden by a cloud, and escapes your dim sight.

Translated by Charles Gordon Browne and James Edward Swallow. From *Nicene and Post-Nicene Fathers,* 2nd Series, edited by Philip Schaff and Henry Wace (New York: Christian Literature Company, 1890–1900), Volume 7, pages 301–303.

Gregory of Nyssa (c.335–394)

From *On "Not Three Gods"*

Basil's brother, Gregory of Nyssa, was a poet and a mystic who lacked Basil's organizational gifts but in treatises like this one shows himself a most sophisticated theologian.

. . . The question you propound to us is no small one, nor such that but small harm will follow if it meets with insufficient treatment. For by the force of the question, we are at first sight compelled to accept one or other of two erroneous opinions, and either to say "there are three Gods," which is unlawful, or not to acknowledge the Godhead of the Son and the Holy Spirit, which is impious and absurd.

The argument which you state is something like this: Peter, James, and John, being in one human nature, are called three men: and there

is no absurdity in describing those who are united in nature, if they
are more than one, by the plural number of the name derived from
their nature. If, then, in the above case, custom admits this, and no
one forbids us to speak of those who are two as two, or those who
are more than two as three, how is it that in the case of our statements of the mysteries of the Faith, though confessing the Three
Persons, and acknowledging no difference of nature between them,
we are in some sense at variance with our confession, when we say
that the Godhead of the Father and of the Son and of the Holy Ghost
is one, and yet forbid men to say "there are three Gods"? . . .

We say, then, to begin with, that the practice of calling those who
are not divided in nature by the very name of their common nature
in the plural, and saying they are "many men," is a customary abuse
of language, and that it would be much the same thing to say they
are "many human natures." And the truth of this we may see from
the following instance. When we address any one, we do not call him
by the name of his nature, in order that no confusion may result from
the community of the name, as would happen if every one of those
who hear it were to think that he himself was the person addressed,
because the call is made not by the proper appellation but by the
common name of their nature: but we separate him from the multitude by using that name which belongs to him as his own;—that, I
mean, which signifies the particular subject. Thus there are many
who have shared in the nature—many disciples, say, or apostles, or
martyrs—but the man in them all is one; since, as has been said, the
term "man" does not belong to the nature of the individual as such,
but to that which is common. For Luke is a man, or Stephen is a man;
but it does not follow that if any one is a man he is therefore Luke
or Stephen: but the idea of the persons admits of that separation
which is made by the peculiar attributes considered in each severally,
and when they are combined is presented to us by means of number;
yet their nature is one, at union in itself, and an absolutely indivisible
unit, not capable of increase by addition or of diminution by subtrac-
tion, but in its essence being and continually remaining one, inseparable even though it appear in plurality, continuous, complete, and
not divided with the individuals who participate in it. And as we
speak of a people, or a mob, or an army, or an assembly in the
singular in every case, while each of these is conceived as being in
plurality, so according to the more accurate expression, "man"
would be said to be one, even though those who are exhibited to us
in the same nature make up a plurality. Thus it would be much better

to correct our erroneous habit, so as no longer to extend to a plurality the name of the nature, than by our bondage to habit to transfer to our statements concerning God the error which exists in the above case. But since the correction of the habit is impracticable (for how could you persuade any one not to speak of those who are exhibited in the same nature as "many men"?—indeed, in every case habit is a thing hard to change), we are not so far wrong in not going contrary to the prevailing habit in the case of the lower nature, since no harm results from the mistaken use of the name: but in the case of the statement concerning the Divine nature the various use of terms is no longer so free from danger. . . . Therefore we must confess one God, according to the testimony of Scripture, "Hear, O Israel, the Lord thy God is one Lord," even though the name of Godhead extends through the Holy Trinity. . . .

But some one will say that the proof of our argument does not yet regard the question. For even if it were granted that the name of "Godhead" is a common name of the nature, it would not be established that we should not speak of "Gods": but by these arguments, on the contrary, we are compelled to speak of "Gods": for we find in the custom of mankind that not only those who are partakers in the same nature, but even any who may be of the same business, are not, when they are many, spoken of in the singular; as we speak of "many orators," or "surveyors," or "farmers," or "shoemakers," and so in all other cases. If, indeed, Godhead were an appellation of nature, it would be more proper, according to the argument laid down, to include the Three Persons in the singular number, and to speak of "One God," by reason of the inseparability and indivisibility of the nature: but since it has been established by what has been said, that the term "Godhead" is significant of operation, and not of nature, the argument from what has been advanced seems to turn to the contrary conclusion, that we ought therefore all the more to call those "three Gods" who are contemplated in the same operation, as they say that one would speak of "three philosophers" or "orators," or any other name derived from a business when those who take part in the same business are more than one. . . .

For instance, supposing the case of several rhetoricians, their pursuit, being one, has the same name in the numerous cases: but each of those who follow it works by himself, this one pleading on his own account, and that on his own account. Thus, since among men the action of each in the same pursuits is discriminated, they are properly called many, since each of them is separated from the others within his own environment, according to the special character of his operation. But in the case of the Divine nature we do not similarly learn that the Father does anything by Himself in which the Son does not work conjointly, or again that the Son has any special operation apart from the Holy Spirit; but every operation which extends from God to the Creation, and is named according to our variable conceptions of it, has its origin from the Father, and proceeds through the Son, and is perfected in the Holy Spirit. For this reason the name derived from the operation is not divided with regard to the number of those who fulfil it, because the action of each concerning anything is not separate and peculiar. . . .

But if it pleases our adversaries to say that the significance of the term is not operation, but nature, we shall fall back upon our original argument, that custom applies the name of a nature to denote multitude erroneously: since according to true reasoning neither diminution nor increase attaches to any nature, when it is contemplated in a larger or smaller number. For it is only those things which are contemplated in their individual circumscription which are enumerated by way of addition. Now this circumscription is noted by bodily appearance, and size, and place, and difference in figure and color, and that which is contemplated apart from these conditions is free from the circumscription which is formed by such categories. That which is not thus circumscribed is not enumerated, and that which is not enumerated cannot be contemplated in multitude. For we say that gold, even though it be cut into many figures, is one, and is so spoken of, but we speak of many coins or many staters,* without finding any multiplication of the nature of gold by the number of staters; and for this reason we speak of gold, when it is contemplated in greater bulk, either in plate or in coin, as "much," but we do not speak of it as "many golds" on account of the multitude of the material. . . .

The Father is God: the Son is God: and yet by the same proclamation God is One, because no difference either of nature or of operation is contemplated in the Godhead.

Translated by William Moore. From *Nicene and Post-Nicene Fathers,* 2nd Series, edited by Philip Schaff and Henry Wace (New York: Christian Literature Company, 1890–1900), Volume 5, pages 331–336.

---

*A type of coin.

Apollinaris of Laodicea (c.300–c.390)

From *On the Union in Christ of the Body with the Godhead*

Apollinaris was a friend and supporter of Athanasius. He developed the Alexandrian "Logos-flesh" Christology in which the Divine Word replaced the human mind of Christ to its full explicitness. Particularly after the death of Athanasius in 373, Apollinaris' views became the center of dramatic controversy.

The confession is that in him the creature is in unity with the uncreated, while the uncreated is commingled with the creature, so that one nature is constituted out of the parts severally, and the Word contributes a special energy to the two together with the divine perfection. The same thing happens in the case of the ordinary man, made up as he is of two incomplete parts which together fill out one nature and are signified by one name; for at the same time the whole is called "flesh" without the soul's being thereby stripped away and the whole is styled "soul" without the body's being stripped away (if, indeed, it is something else alongside the soul). So the God who became human, the Lord and ruler of all that comes to be, may have come to be of a woman, yet he is Lord. He may have been formed after the fashion of slaves, yet he is Spirit. He may be proclaimed as flesh because of his union with the flesh, yet according to the apostle he is not a human being; and though he is preached as human by the same apostle, yet he calls the whole Christ invisible God transformed by a visible body, uncreated God made manifest in a created garment. He emptied himself after the fashion of a slave, but in his divine essence he is unemptied and unaltered and undiminished (for no alteration can affect the divine nature), neither is he decreased or increased.

When he says, "Glorify me," this utterance stems from the body, and the glorification touches the body, but the reference is to Christ as a whole, because the whole is one. He adds, ". . . with the glory which I possessed with you before the existence of the world" [John 17:5] and manifests the eternally glorious Godhead, but though this expression peculiarly befits the Godhead, it was spoken inclusively with reference to the whole. Thus he is both coessential with God in the invisible Spirit (the flesh being comprehended in the title because it has been united to that which is coessential with God), and again coessential with men (the Godhead being comprehended with the body because it has been united to what is coessential with us). And the nature of the flesh is not altered by its union with what is coessential with God and by its participation in the title of *homoousios,* even as the nature of the Godhead is not changed by its participation of a human body and by bearing the name of a flesh coessential with us.

The passages that follow come from surviving fragments of Apollinaris' other works.

9. If the same one is a complete human being and God as well, and the pious spirit does not worship a human being but worships God, it will be found both worshiping and not worshiping the same person—which is impossible. Moreover, humanity itself does not judge itself to be an object of worship . . . but God knows himself to be an object of worship. Yet it is inconceivable that the same person should both know himself to be an object of worship and not know it. Therefore, it is inconceivable that the same person should be both God and an entire man. Rather, he exists in the singleness of an incarnate divine nature which is commingled [with flesh], with the result that worshipers bend their attention to God inseparable from his flesh and not to one who is worshiped and one who is not. . . .

22. But the flesh is not soulless, for it is said to fight against the spirit and to resist the law of the intellect, and we say that even the bodies of beasts without reason are endowed with soul.

25. So Christ, having God as his spirit—his intellect—together with soul and body, is rightly called "the human being from heaven."

45. He is not a human being but is like a human being, since he is not coessential with humanity in his highest part.

69. For he would not have been born in the likeness of a human being unless, like a human being, he was in fact an incarnate intellect.

74. If together with God, who is intellect, there was also a human intellect in Christ, then the work of the incarnation is not accomplished in him. But if the work of the incarnation is not accomplished in the self-moved and undetermined intellect, then this work, which is the destruction of sin, is accomplished in the flesh, which is moved from without and energized by the divine Intellect. The self-moved intellect within us shares in the destruction of sin insofar as it assimilates itself to Christ.

76. Therefore, the human race is saved not by the assumption of an intellect and of a whole human being but by the assumption of flesh, whose nature it is to be ruled. What was needed was unchangeable Intellect which did not fall under the domination of the flesh on account of its weakness of understanding but which adapted the flesh to itself without force.

From Apollinaris of Laodicea, "On the Union in Christ of the Body with the Godhead," in *The Christological Controversy,* translated and edited by Richard A. Norris, Jr. (Sources of Early Christian Thought), pages 104–105, 107–109. Copyright © 1980 by Fortress Press. Used by permission of the publisher.

Theodore of Mopsuestia (c.350–428)

From *On the Nicene Creed*

Theodore was the greatest theologian of the "two-natures" Christology of the school of Antioch. This selection shows both Theodore's criticisms of the Alexandrian tradition and also the theme that Nestorius later developed—the firm distinction between Christ's humanity and divinity.

Chapter 3. . . . Let us quote and examine also the words uttered by our blessed Fathers in the profession of faith concerning the Son: *and in one Lord Jesus Christ the Only Begotten Son of God, the first-born of all creatures.* . . . In order to include in their sentence the human nature which was assumed for our salvation they said: *In one Lord Jesus Christ.* This name is that of the man whom God put on, as the angel said: "She shall bring forth a Son whose name shall be called 'Jesus' " [Matt. 1:21; Luke 1:31]. They added also the word *Christ* in order to allude to the Holy Spirit, as it is written: "Jesus of Nazareth whom God anointed with the Holy Ghost and with power" [Acts 10:38]. And He is God because of the close union with that Divine nature which is truly God.

In this same way our blessed Fathers who assembled in that wonderful Council of the Catholic Church [of Nicaea] first spoke, like Paul, of Divine nature while coupling with it a word which denotes the form of humanity which He took upon Him [Phil.2:7] and said: *And in one Lord Jesus Christ the Only Begotten Son of God, the first-born of all creatures.* It is thus that they wished to teach mankind when they spoke of the Divine nature of the Son. His humanity, in which is Divine nature, is also made known and proclaimed in it, according to the saying of the blessed Paul: "God was manifest in the flesh" [1 Tim. 3:16]. . . .

After saying these and showing the Divine nature and the human nature which God put on, they added: *The "Only Begotten Son," the "first-born" of all creatures.* With these two words they alluded to the two natures, and by the difference between the words they made us understand the difference between the natures. From the fact also that they referred both words to the one person of the Son they showed us the close union between the two natures. They did not make use of these words out of their own head but they took them from the teaching of Holy Writ. The Blessed Paul said: "Of whom Christ in the flesh, who is God over all" [Rom. 9:5], not that He is God by nature from the fact that He is of the House of David in the flesh, but he said "in the flesh" in order to indicate the human nature that was assumed. He said "God over all" in order to indicate the Divine nature which is higher than all, and which is the Lord. He used both words of one person in order to teach the close union of the two natures, and to make manifest the majesty and the honour that came to the man who was assumed by God who put Him on. . . .

Chapter 5. . . . It is with justice, therefore, that our blessed Fathers said: *He was incarnate and became a man* in order to show that He was a man, as the blessed Paul testifies, and that He fulfilled this Economy for the salvation of all. It is with justice then that our blessed Fathers made use of this word in the profession of faith for the refutation of the error of the heretics, while conforming with the true belief of the Church. And on account of the numerous schisms that had taken place among men concerning that ineffable Economy and concerning the man whom our Lord assumed, they rightly made use of the sentence: *He was incarnate and became a man.*

The Marcionites and the Manicheans together with the followers of Valentinus* and the rest of the heretics who were affected with a like malady, say that our Lord did not assume any of our natures, either of the body or the soul, but that He was a phantasm that struck the eyes of men like the form of the visions which the prophets saw and the apparition seen by Abraham of three men of whom none had a corporeal nature but who were only in appearance men who per-

---

*Valentinus was a second-century Egyptian Gnostic. For Marcion, see Chapter 1; for the Manicheans, see Chapter 5.

formed human acts, walked, talked, were washed, ate, and drank. They say that in this same way our Lord did not assume any body but that He was only in appearance a man who performed and felt everything according to the requirements of men, while the one who was seen had no human nature but was only seen in appearance to be so, and that in reality He felt nothing but only the onlookers believed that He was feeling.

The partisans of Arius and Eunomius,* however, say that He assumed a body but not a soul, and that the nature of the Godhead took the place of the soul. They lowered the Divine nature of the Only Begotten to the extent that from the greatness of its nature it moved and performed the acts of the soul and imprisoned itself in the body and did everything for its sustenance. Lo, if the Godhead had replaced the soul He would not have been hungry or thirsty, nor would He have tired or been in need of food. All these things befall the body because of its weakness, as the soul is not able to satisfy its wants, but does for it only those things that belong to itself according to the nature given to it by God. . . .

Our blessed Fathers said that He became incarnate so that you might understand that He assumed a complete man, who was a man not only in appearance but a man in a true human nature, and that you might believe that He assumed not only the body but the whole man who is composed of a body and of an immortal and rational soul. It is such a man that He assumed for our salvation and it is through Him that He effected salvation for our life. . . .

Chapter 6. . . . In their profession of faith our blessed Fathers . . . do not teach that the Divine nature of the Only begotten was born of a woman as if it had its beginning in her, because they did not say that the one who was born of His Father before all the worlds and who is eternally from Him and with Him had His beginning from Mary, but they followed the Sacred Books which speak differently of natures while referring [them] to one *prosōpon* † on account of the close union that took place between them, so that they might not be believed that they were separating the perfect union between the one who was assumed and the one who assumed. . . .

It is not Divine nature that received death, but it is clear that it

---

*A fourth-century Arian bishop.

†Person.

was that man who was assumed as a temple to God the Word, [a temple] which was dissolved and then raised by the one who had assumed it. And after the Crucifixion it was not Divine nature that was raised but the temple which was assumed, which rose from the dead, ascended to heaven and sat at the right hand of God: nor is it to Divine nature—the cause of everything—that it was given that every one should worship it and every knee should bow, but worship was granted to the form of a servant which did not in its nature possess [the right to be worshipped].

From Theodore of Mopsuestia, *On the Nicene Creed,* translated by A. Mingana, in *Woodbrooke Studies,* vol. 5 (Cambridge: W. Heffer & Sons, 1932), pages 35–37, 54–55, 60, 63–64, 66. Used by permission of the publisher.

Nestorius (c.381–c.451)

From *First Sermon Against the* Theotokos

Nestorius became archbishop or patriarch of Constantinople in 428 and soon faced a concerted campaign against him by Cyril of Alexandria. As this selection indicates, Nestorius so emphasized the two natures of Christ that he risked losing sight of their union—and he offended popular piety by denying that Mary was the theotokos *or bearer of God.*

The human race was adorned with ten thousand gifts when it was dignified by a gift which was furthest away and nearest to hand—the Lord's incarnation. Because humanity is the image of the divine nature, but the devil overthrew this image and cast it down into corruption, God grieved over his image as a king might grieve over his statue, and renewed the ruined likeness. Without male seed, he fashioned from the Virgin a nature like Adam's (who was himself formed without male seed) and through a human being brought about the revival of the human race. "Since," Paul says, "death came through a human being, through a human being also came the resurrection of the dead" [1 Cor. 15:21].

Let those people pay attention to these words who, blinded with regard to the dispensation of the Lord's incarnation, "do not understand either the words they employ or the things they are talking about" [1 Tim. 1:7]. I mean those who, as we have now learned, are always inquiring among us now this way and now that: "Is Mary *theotokos,"* they say (that is, the bearer or mother of God), "or is she on the contrary *anthrōpotokos"* (that is, the bearer or mother of a human being)?

Does God have a mother? A Greek without reproach introducing mothers for the gods! Is Paul then a liar when he says of the deity of Christ, "without father, without mother, without genealogy" [Heb. 7:3]? Mary, my friend, did not give birth to the Godhead (for "what is born of the flesh is flesh" [John 3:6]). A creature did not produce him who is uncreatable. The Father has not just recently generated God the Logos from the Virgin (for "in the beginning was the Logos," as John [John 1:1] says). A creature did not produce the Creator, rather she gave birth to the human being, the instrument of the Godhead. The Holy Spirit did not create God the Logos (for "what is born of her is of the Holy Spirit" [Matt. 1:20]). Rather, he formed out of the Virgin a temple for God the Logos, a temple in which he dwelt.

Moreover, the incarnate God did not die; he raised up the one in whom he was incarnate. He stooped down to raise up what had collapsed, but he did not fall ("The Lord looked down from heaven over the sons of men" [Ps. 14:2]). Nor, because he stooped to lift up the guilty who had fallen, may he be disparaged as if he himself had sunk to the ground. God saw the ruined nature, and the power of the Godhead took hold of it in its shattered state. God held on to it while himself remaining what he had been, and lifted it up high. . . .

Humanity owed God an unblamable life lived without complaint, but it fell short in carrying out its duty. . . .

What, then, of the Lord Christ? Perceiving that the human race was tied up in its sins and unworthy of restoration, he did not dissolve the debt by an order, lest mercy violate justice. And the apostle Paul is a witness of this when he exclaims, "Christ, whom God set forth as an expiation through faith in his blood to demonstrate his justice" [Rom. 3:25]—that mercy, he means, may be shown to be just and not something bestowed without judgment here and there and how you please.

Consequently, Christ assumed the person of the debt-ridden nature and by its mediation paid the debt back as a son of Adam, for it was obligatory that the one who dissolved the debt come from the same race as he who had once contracted it. The debt had its start from a woman, and the remission had its start from a woman. . . .

Now see our nature, in God's company in Christ, pleading its case against the devil and employing the following valid arguments: "I am oppressed by wrong, O most just judge. The wicked devil attacks me; he uses my powerlessness against me in a manifest assertion of unjust power. Be it so that he handed the former Adam over to death because he was the occasion of [Adam's] sinning; and now the Second Adam, whom you have formed out of a virgin—for what offense, O king, has he crucified him? . . . show yourself a just judge on my behalf. You have been angry at me by reason of Adam's transgression. I beseech you, on his behalf, to be favorable, if it be the case that you have joined to you an Adam who is without sin. Be it so that on account of the former Adam you have handed me over to corruption; on this one's account, make me partake of incorruption. Both of them have my nature. As I shared in the death of the former, so I shall become a participant in the immortal life of the second." . . .

Just as the devil held the protoplast's sin against his whole posterity and sustained the original charge, so too, when our nature had in Christ come into possession of the guiltless firstfruits of its total body, it struggled against the devil and conquered, by means of the very weapons which the adversary had used previously. . . . Our nature, having been put on by Christ like a garment, intervenes on our behalf, being entirely free from all sin and contending by appeal to its blameless origin, just as the Adam who was formed earlier brought punishment upon his race by reason of his sin. This was the opportunity which belonged to the assumed man, as a human being to dissolve, by means of the flesh, that corruption which arose by means of the flesh. The third-day burial belonged to this man, not to the deity. His feet were fastened down by nails; he is the one whom the Holy Spirit formed in the womb. . . .

Attend to what is said here. That which was formed in the womb is not in itself God. That which was created by the Spirit was not in itself God. That which was buried in the tomb was not in itself God. If that were the case, we should manifestly be worshipers of a human being and worshipers of the dead. But since God is within the one who was assumed, the one who was assumed is styled God because of the one who assumed him.

From *The Christological Controversy,* translated and edited by Richard A. Norris, Jr. (Sources of Early Christian Thought), pages 124–130, Copyright © 1980 by Fortress Press. Used by permission of the publisher.

Cyril of Alexandria (d. 444)

From *First Letter to Nestorius*

Ambitious and scheming, Cyril is not one of the more attractive figures in the history of theology, but as Patriarch of Alexandria for many years he made an important contribution to that history. Unlike Apollinaris, he admitted that Christ had a human mind as well as a human body. But in his earlier works, such as the one that follows, written in 429, he rejected the idea that after the Incarnation there were still "two natures," human and divine. Only belief in "one nature," he thought, preserved Christ's unity. Later he retreated even from that position and acknowledged that, with careful qualifications, one could speak of two natures, as long as the properties of one could be attributed to the other, so that, for example, one could call Mary the Mother of God even though Christ's birth had to do directly with his human nature.

Confessing the Word to be made one with the flesh according to substance, we adore one Son and Lord Jesus Christ: we do not divide the God from the man, nor separate him into parts, as though the two natures were mutually united in him only through a sharing of dignity and authority (for that is a novelty and nothing else), neither do we give separately to the Word of God the name Christ and the same name separately to a different one born of a woman; but we know only one Christ, the Word from God the Father with his own Flesh. For as man he was anointed with us, although it is he himself who gives the Spirit to those who are worthy and not in measure, according to the saying of the blessed Evangelist John.

But we do not say that the Word of God dwelt in him as in a common man born of the holy Virgin, lest Christ be thought of as a God-bearing man; for although the Word tabernacled among us, it is also said that in Christ "dwelt all the fulness of the Godhead bodily"; but we understand that he became flesh, not just as he is said to dwell in the saints, but we define that that tabernacling in him was according to equality. But being made one *kata physin* [according to nature] and not converted into flesh, he made his indwelling in such a way, as we may say that the soul of man does in his own body.

One therefore is Christ both Son and Lord, not as if a man had attained only such a conjunction with God as consists in a unity of dignity alone or of authority. For it is not equality of honor which unites natures; for then Peter and John, who were of equal honor with each other, being both Apostles and holy disciples, [would have been one, and] yet the two are not one. . . . We deprecate the term of "junction" as not having sufficiently signified the oneness. . . .

We confess that he is the Son, begotten of God the Father, and Only-begotten God; and although according to his own nature he was not subject to suffering, yet he suffered for us in the flesh according to the Scriptures, and although impassible, yet in his Crucified Body he made his own the suffering of his own flesh; and by the grace of God he tasted death for all: he gave his own Body thereto, although he was by nature himself the life and the resurrection, in order that, having trodden down death by his unspeakable power, first in his own flesh, he might become the first born from the dead, and the first-fruits of them that slept. . . .

For if it is necessary to believe that being by nature God, he became flesh, that is, a man endowed with a reasonable soul, what reason can certain ones have to be ashamed of this language about him, which is suitable to him as man? For if he should reject the words suitable to him as man, who compelled him to become man like us? And as he humbled himself to a voluntary abasement for us, for what cause can any one reject the words suitable to such abasement? . . .

And since the holy Virgin brought forth corporeally God made one with flesh according to nature, for this reason we also call her Mother of God, not as if the nature of the Word had the beginning of its existence from the flesh.

For "In the beginning was the Word, and the Word was God, and the Word was with God," and he is the Maker of the ages, coeternal with the Father, and Creator of all; but, as we have already said, since he united to himself hypostatically human nature from her womb, also he subjected himself to birth as man, not as needing necessarily in his own nature birth in time and in these last times of the world, but in order that he might bless the beginning of our existence, and that that which sent the earthly bodies of our whole race to death, might lose its power for the future by his being born of a woman in the flesh.

Translated by Henry R. Percival. From *Nicene and Post-Nicene Fathers*, 2nd Series, edited by Philip Schaff and Henry Wace (New York: Christian Literature Company, 1890–1900), Volume 14, pages 201–205.

Pope Leo I (c.400–461)

From *The Tome of Leo*

Leo, who was Pope from 440 to 461, is justifiably known as "Leo the Great." He somehow talked Attila the Hun out of attacking Rome, and he had an important influence on theology. In the debates between Cyril and the followers of Nestorius, someone appealed to Leo for advice, and he sent this letter to the Council of Ephesus in 449. It arguably avoids some of the tough questions Greek theologians had been facing, but it does offer the language of a workable compromise. Cyril's followers had control of the council and prevented the letter from being read, but it became one of the bases for the settlement at the Council of Chalcedon two years later.

. . . The whole body of the faithful profess that they "believe in God the Father Almighty, and in Jesus Christ his only Son our Lord, who was born of the Holy Ghost and the Virgin Mary." By which three clauses the engines of almost all heretics are shattered. For when God is believed to be both "Almighty" and "Father," it is proved that the Son is everlasting together with himself, differing in nothing from the Father, because he was born as "God from God," Almighty from Almighty, Coeternal from Eternal; not later in time, not inferior in power, not unlike him in glory, not divided from him in essence, but the same Only-begotten and Everlasting Son of an Everlasting Parent was "born of the Holy Ghost and the Virgin Mary." This birth in time in no way detracted from, in no way added to, that divine and everlasting birth; but expended itself wholly in the work of restoring man, who had been deceived; so that it might both overcome death, and by its power "destroy the devil who had the power of death." For we could not have overcome the author of sin and of death, unless he who could neither be contaminated by sin, nor detained by death, had taken upon himself our nature, and made it his own. For, in fact, he was "conceived of the Holy Ghost" within the womb of a Virgin Mother, who bore him as she had conceived him, without loss of virginity. . . .

For it was the Holy Ghost who gave fecundity to the Virgin, but it was from a body that a real body was derived; and "when Wisdom was building herself a house," the "Word was made flesh, and dwelt among us," that is, in that flesh which he assumed from a human being, and which he animated with the spirit of rational life. Accordingly, while the distinctness of both natures and substances was preserved, and both met in one Person, lowliness was assumed by majesty, weakness by power, mortality by eternity; and, in order to pay the debt of our condition, the inviolable nature was united to the passible, so that as the appropriate remedy for our ills, one and the same "Mediator between God and man, the Man Christ Jesus," might from one element be capable of dying and also from the other be incapable. Therefore in the entire and perfect nature of every man was born very God, whole in what was his, whole in what was ours. By "ours" we mean what the Creator forms in us at the beginning and what he assumed in order to restore; for of that which the deceiver brought in, and man, thus deceived, admitted, there was not a trace in the Savior; and the fact that he took on himself a share in our infirmities did not make him a partaker in our transgressions. He assumed "the form of a servant" without the defilement of sin, enriching what was human, not impairing what was divine: because that "emptying of himself," whereby the Invisible made himself visible, and the Creator and Lord of all things willed to be one among mortals, was a stooping down in compassion, not a failure of power. Accordingly, the same who, remaining in the form of God, made man, was made man in the form of a servant. For each of the natures retains its proper character without defect; and as the form of God does not take away the form of a servant, so the form of a servant does not impair the form of God. . . .

What was assumed from the Lord's mother was nature, not fault; nor does the wondrousness of the nativity of our Lord Jesus Christ, as born of a Virgin's womb, imply that his nature is unlike ours. For the selfsame who is very God, is also very man; and there is no illusion in this union, while the lowliness of man and the loftiness of Godhead meet together. For as "God" is not changed by the compassion [exhibited], so "Man" is not consumed by the dignity [bestowed]. For each "form" does the acts which belong to it, in communion with the other; the Word, that is, performing what belongs to the Word, and the flesh carrying out what belongs to the flesh; the one of these shines out in miracles, the other succumbs to injuries. And as the Word does not withdraw from equality with the Father in glory, so the flesh does not abandon the nature of our kind. For, as we must often be saying, he is one and the same, truly Son of God, and truly Son of Man.

Translated by Henry R. Percival. From *Nicene and Post-Nicene Fathers*, 2nd Series, edited by Philip Schaff and Henry Wace (New York: Christian Literature Company, 1890–1900), Volume 14, pages 254–256.

The Definition of Chalcedon

Meeting in 451, the Council of Chalcedon managed a careful compromise between the dangers of Apollinarianism and Nestorianism, acknowledging Christ "in two natures" but emphasizing the close union of those natures in one person.

Following, then, the holy fathers, we unite in teaching all men to confess the one and only Son, our Lord Jesus Christ. This selfsame one is perfect both in deity and also in human-ness; this selfsame one is also actually God and actually man, with a rational soul and a body. He is of the same reality as God as far as his deity is concerned and of the same reality as we are ourselves as far as his human-ness is concerned; thus like us in all respects, sin only excepted. Before time began he was begotten of the Father, in respect of his deity, and now in these "last days," for us and on behalf of our salvation, this selfsame one was born of Mary the virgin, who is God-bearer in respect of his human-ness.

[We also teach] that we apprehend this one and only Christ—Son, Lord, only-begotten—in two natures; [and we do this] without confusing the two natures, without transmuting one nature into the other, without dividing them into two separate categories, without contrasting them according to area or function. The distinctiveness of each nature is not nullified by the union. Instead, the "properties" of each nature are conserved and both natures concur in one "person" and in one *hypostasis.* They are not divided or cut into two *prosōpa* [persons], but are together the one and only and only-begotten Logos of God, the Lord Jesus Christ. Thus have the prophets of old testified; thus the Lord Jesus Christ himself taught us; thus the Symbol of the Fathers has handed down to us.

Translated by Albert C. Outler. From *Creeds of the Churches,* edited by John H. Leith (Chicago: Aldine Publishing Company, 1963; 3rd edition, Atlanta: John Knox Press, 1982), pages 35–36. Copyright © 1963 by John H. Leith. Used by permission of the editor.

CHAPTER 4

Eastern Theology
After Chalcedon

The Council of Chalcedon in 451 addressed a Christian community that stretched from Spain and Britain to the Middle East and beyond, but in the years following, as the Roman Empire declined and divided, communication gradually broke down between the Greek-speaking East and the Latin-speaking West, and the two halves of the Christian world pursued different theological agendas. The debate about grace, so central in the West after Augustine, for instance, played a much smaller role in the East. There the continuing strength of the emperor raised a special set of questions about the relation of church and state, theologians continued to debate technical questions about Christology, and mysticism and the "negative theology" related to it became a central theological theme. In subsequent centuries debates over iconoclasm and hesychasm, issues almost unknown in the West, deeply divided the Eastern church.

Chalcedon had declared that even after the Incarnation Christ retained two natures, human and divine, but Monophysite ("one-nature") Christians remained a strong force in the East, and a number of emperors sought a theological compromise in order to help hold the Empire together. In the 600s the search for such a compromise shifted to the question of Christ's wills. The Monothelites ("one-will") proposed that, however things stood with his natures, at any rate the human and divine were so united in Christ that he had only one will. In the 630s Pope Honorius I seemed to have supported this position, but about fifty years later one of his successors, Pope Agatho, rejected it, and that rejection stood firm in the West. In the East, however, emperors continued to seek compromises, and in 647 or 648 Constans II promulgated an edict called the *Typos,* which ordered everyone to stop discussing the question of Christ's wills altogether and simply repeat the formulas of the early councils. The great theologian Maximus the Confessor, who opposed the *Typos* in the late 600s, was both defending the Christology of two wills and opposing imperial interference in theological questions.

Theological independence came under attack once again in the 700s when several emperors advocated the cause of iconoclasm, the belief that the images of Christ, Mary, and the saints that played so important a role in the worship of the Eastern churches were idols that ought to be destroyed. John of Damascus in the 700s and Theodore the Studite in the 800s developed the theological tradition of Eastern Christianity generally and opposed iconoclasm and imperial interference in theology in particular.

Maximus, John, and Theodore were all monks and mystics, and reference to the encounter with God in mystic experience often played an important role in Eastern theology. It was often connected with the tradition of negative theology—the belief that one cannot say what God is but only what God is not. If God cannot be described, after all, it could be argued that one can know him only through direct experience. Around the year 1000, monks on Mount Athos in northern Greece focused questions about the nature of such experience in the development of the hesychast movement. The hesychasts used special techniques for prayer and claimed to experience the "uncreated light," which the disciples had seen surround Jesus at the Transfiguration. In the 1300s Gregory Palamas defended a modified hesychasm and summarized much of Eastern theology in a magisterial way that calls for comparison with his near contemporary, Thomas Aquinas.

By the time of Gregory Palamas, Eastern and Western churches had clearly separated. While they began drifting apart in the 400s, an official split came temporarily in the 800s and finally in 1054, when the pope and the patriarch of Constantinople excommunicated each other. Many issues of custom and practice contributed to the division, but the chief point of theological contention was that when Latin-speaking Christians recited the Nicene Creed and spoke of the Holy Spirit proceeding from the Father, they added the phrase "and the Son," which had not been part of the revision of the Nicene Creed at the Second Council of Constantinople. The Greek-speaking East took that *"filioque"* as a heretical innovation.

Pope Agatho (c.577–681)

From *Letter to the Emperor*

Agatho was Pope from 678 to 681 and gave crucial support to the Third Council of Constantinople's condemnation of Monothelitism in 680, a particularly delicate business since Pope Honorius I (pope from 625 to 638) had supported the Monothelites.

. . . The Apostolic Church of Christ, the spiritual mother of your God-founded empire, confesses one Jesus Christ our Lord existing of and in two natures, and she maintains that his two natures, to wit, the divine and the human, exist in him unconfused even after their inseparable union, and she acknowledges that each of these natures of Christ is perfect in the proprieties of its nature, and she confesses that all things belonging to the proprieties of the natures are double, because the same our Lord Jesus Christ himself is both perfect God and perfect man, of two and in two natures: and after his wonderful incarnation, his deity cannot be thought of without his humanity, nor his humanity without his deity. Consequently, therefore, according to the rule of the holy Catholic and Apostolic Church of Christ, she also confesses and preaches that there are in him two natural wills and two natural operations. For if anybody should mean a personal will, when in the holy Trinity there are said to be three Persons, it would be necessary that there should be asserted three personal wills, and three personal operations (which is absurd and truly profane). Since, as the truth of the Christian faith holds, the will is natural, where the one nature of the holy and inseparable Trinity is spoken of, it must be consistently understood that there is one natural will, and one natural operation. But when in truth we confess that in the one person of our Lord Jesus Christ the mediator between God and man, there are two natures (that is to say the divine and the human), even after his admirable union, just as we canonically confess the two natures of one and the same person, so too we confess his two natural wills and two natural operations. . . .

Our Lord Jesus Christ himself, who is true and perfect God, and true and perfect man, in his holy Gospels shows forth in some instances human things, in others divine, and still in others both together, making a manifestation concerning himself in order that he might instruct his faithful to believe and preach that he is both true God and true man. Thus as man he prays to the Father to take away the cup of suffering, because in him our human nature was complete, sin only excepted, "Father, if it be possible, let this cup pass from me; nevertheless not as I will, but as thou wilt." And in another passage, "Not my will, but thine be done." . . .

The words our Lord used in his prayer, "Not my will," pertain to his humanity; through which also he is said, according to the teaching of Blessed Paul the Apostle of the Gentiles, to have "become obedient unto death, even the death of the Cross." Wherefore also it is taught us that he was obedient to his parents, which must piously be understood to refer to his voluntary obedience, not according to his divinity (by which he governs all things), but according to his humanity, by which he spontaneously submitted himself to his parents. . . .

From all which it is evident that he had a human will by which he obeyed his Father, and that he had in himself this same human will immaculate from all sin, as true God and man.

Translated by Henry R. Percival. From *Nicene and Post-Nicene Fathers,* 2nd Series, edited by Philip Schaff and Henry Wace (New York: Christian Literature Company, 1890–1900), Volume 14, pages 332–334.

Maximus the Confessor (c.580–662)

From *The Trial of Maximus*

Maximus led the opposition to imperial compromises with the Monophysites, such as the edict of Constans II, the Typos. *This selection recounts the story of Maximus' trial, beginning with the testimony of one of the witnesses against him. After the trial his tongue and right hand were cut off, and he was exiled under such severe conditions that he died soon afterward.*

4. After this one they led in a fourth person, Gregory the son of Photinus, who said, "I went to the cell of the abbot Maximus in Rome and when I mentioned that the emperor is also a priest the monk Anastasius his disciple said, 'He should not be considered a priest.' " The servant of God* said right off to him, "Fear God, lord Gregory, my fellow servant did not say anything at all in this conversation on this matter." And he threw himself upon the ground, saying to the senate, "Bear with your servant and I will tell you all as it took place, and he shall convict me if I lie. My lord Gregory on his arrival in Rome deigned to come to your servant's cell. Upon seeing him I prostrated myself upon the earth as is my custom and greeted him. And having kissed him I said to him after we had seated ourselves, 'What is the reason for the welcome presence of my lord?' And he said, 'Our good and God-established lord, having charge of

---

*Maximus.

the peace of the saints of God's churches, has issued an order to the God-honored Pope, sending an offering as well to St. Peter, urging him to establish communion with the patriarch of Constantinople; his venerable majesty deigned that this order be sent through your humble servant.' And I said, 'Glory to God who made you worthy of such a ministry. Now on what formula has his divinely crowned serenity ordered the union to come about? Tell me if you know.' And you said, 'On the Typos.' And I said, 'This, I think, is an impossible thing; for the Romans will not consent that the illuminating statements of the holy Fathers be annulled together with the voices of impure heretics, or that the truth be extinguished with falsehood, or that the light disappear along with the darkness. For nothing will remain for us to worship if we annul the sayings taught by God.' And you said, 'The Typos does not prescribe a denial of the holy statements but rather a silence in order to arrange a peace.' And I said, 'Silence according to the divine Scripture is denial as well. For God said through David, "There is no speech, nor are there words whose sounds are not heard" [Ps. 19:3]. Therefore unless the words concerning God can be spoken and heard then neither do they exist, according to Scripture. . . . But if the saving faith should be removed along with heresy for the sake of an arrangement, then the arrangement is a thorough separation from God and not a unity with God. For tomorrow the abominable Jews will say, "Let us arrange a peace with one another and unite, and let us remove circumcision and you baptism and we shall not dispute anymore with each other." Once the Arians put this forward in writing at the time of the great Constantine, saying, "Let us remove the Homoousion and the Heterousion* and let the churches unite." Our God-fearing Fathers did not consent to this; but rather they preferred to be pursued and put to death than to pass over in silence a term indicating the one supersubstantial godhead of the Father, Son, and Holy Spirit. And the great Constantine concurred with those who were putting such suggestions forward, as is recounted by many who diligently wrote of these matters at the time. No emperor was able to convince the inspired Fathers to come to an agreement with the heretics of that time through the use of equivocal terms. Rather they employed clear and fixed terms corresponding to the dogma inquired about, saying

------

*In other words, let us no longer debate whether the Son is of the same substance (*homoousios*) or of a different substance (*heterousios*) with the Father.

in as many words, "It is for the priests to inquire into and define what concerns the saving dogmas of the Catholic Church." ' And you said, 'What, then, is not every Christian emperor also a priest?' And I said, 'He is not, for neither does he stand at the altar nor after the consecration of the bread does he elevate it saying, "Holy things for the holy." Nor does he baptize, or anoint, or lay on hands and make bishops and priests and deacons; nor does he anoint churches, or wear the symbols of the priesthood, the pallium and the Gospel book as the crown and purple robe are symbols of kingship.' " . . .

8. Then they asked, "Is it altogether necessary to speak of wills and energies on the subject of Christ?" He answered, "Altogether necessary if we want to worship in truth, for no being exists without natural activity. Indeed, the holy Fathers say plainly that it is impossible for any nature at all to be or to be known apart from its essential activity. And if there is no such thing as a nature to be or to be known without its essential characteristic activity, how is it possible for Christ to be or be known as truly God and man by nature without the divine and human activities? For according to the Fathers, the lion who loses his roaring ability is no lion at all, and a dog without the power to bark is not a dog. And any other thing which has lost something naturally constitutive of it is not any more what it was." And they said to him, "We know well that this is so; still, do not grieve the emperor who issued the Typos for the sake of peace and that alone, not because he wanted to destroy any of those things understood of Christ but to arrange for the silence of those terms which were causing the dissension."

9. Then casting himself upon the ground with tears, the servant of God said, "Let not the good and pious lord be offended by my lowliness. I cannot grieve God by keeping silent about what he ordered us to speak and confess." . . .

15. . . . And on the next day, which was Sunday, the officials of the Church held a meeting and persuaded the emperor to condemn them to that cruel and inhuman exile and to separate them from each other, the holy old man to Bizya, a city of Thrace, and his disciples to Perberis, at the outer limit of the Roman Empire, unprovided for, naked, without nourishment, lacking every resource of life.

Pseudo-Dionysius the Areopagite (c.500)

From *Mystical Theology*

The works of Pseudo-Dionysius were probably written by a Syrian monk around 500 but were long considered the work of the Dionysius mentioned in Acts 17:34 as a convert of Paul. Therefore, they had great authority in both East and West throughout the Middle Ages, especially as the great text of "negative theology," the tradition that we can speak of God only by indicating what cannot be said.

Chapter 1

O Trinity
  beyond being,
  beyond divinity,
  beyond goodness, and
  guide to Christians in divine wisdom,
direct us to the mystical summits
  more than unknown and beyond light,
  There the simple, absolved, and
    unchanged mysteries of theology
  lie hidden in the darkness beyond light
  of the hidden mystical silence,
there, in the greatest darkness,
  that beyond all that is most evident
  exceedingly illuminates the sightless
    intellects,
  there, in the wholly imperceptible and invisible,
    that beyond all that is most evident
    fills to overflowing the sightless intellects
    with the glories beyond all beauty.
This is my prayer.
And you, dear Timothy,
  in the earnest exercise of
    mystical contemplation, abandon
  all sensation and all intellectual activities
  all that is sensed and intelligible,
  all non-beings and all beings;
thus you will unknowingly be elevated,
  as far as possible,
to the unity of that beyond being and knowledge.

By the irrepressible and absolving ecstasis
  of yourself and of all,
  absolved from all, and
  going away from all,
you will be purely raised up
  to the rays of the divine darkness
  beyond being. . . .

Chapter 3

In the *Divine Names* we have celebrated how God is called good, be-ing, life, wisdom, power, and whatever else pertains to the intelligible divine names. . . .

Now, however, that we are to enter the darkness beyond intellect, you will not find a brief discourse but a complete absence of discourse and intelligibility. In affirmative theology the logos descends from what is above down to the last, and increases according to the measure of the descent towards an analogical multitude. But here, as we ascend from the highest to what lies beyond, the logos is drawn inward according to the measure of the ascent. After all ascent it will be wholly without sound and wholly united to the unspeakable. . . .

Chapter 4

We say this of the cause of all be-ing beyond all:
It is
  not being-less,
not lifeless,
not without reason, not without intellect.
Not body,
not figure, not form,
not what has quality, quantity, or mass,
  not in space,
not visible,
not what has sensible contact,
not what has sensation or what is sensed,
not what has disorder and confusion,
not what is troubled by material passions,
not powerless,
not subjected to what happens to sensibles,
not light in what lacks,

not, and has not, alteration, destruction,
privation, diminution, or anything else
which pertains to what is sensed.

John of Damascus (c.675–c.749)

From *The Orthodox Faith*

John was a court official for a Muslim ruler in Syria (and therefore safe from arrest by Christian emperors), but he retired from the world to the monastic life and wrote perhaps the most important systematic account of the faith of the Eastern church.

Book 1

Chapter 1. "No man hath seen God at any time: the only-begotten Son who is in the bosom of the Father, he hath declared him." The God-head, then, is ineffable and incomprehensible. For "no one knoweth the Father, but the Son: neither doth any one know the Son, but the Father." Furthermore, the Holy Spirit knows the things of God, just as the spirit of man knows what is in man. After the first blessed state of nature, no one has ever known God unless God Himself revealed it to him—not only no man, but not even any of the supramundane powers: the very Cherubim and Seraphim, I mean.

Nevertheless, God has not gone so far as to leave us in complete ignorance, for through nature the knowledge of the existence of God has been revealed by Him to all men. The very creation of its harmony and ordering proclaims the majesty of the divine nature. Indeed, He has given us knowledge of Himself in accordance with our capacity, at first through the Law and the Prophets and then afterwards through His only-begotten Son, our Lord and God and Savior, Jesus Christ. Accordingly, we accept all those things that have been handed down by the Law and the Prophets and the Apostles and the Evangelists, and we know and revere them, and over and above these things we seek nothing else. . . . With these things let us be content and in them let us abide and let us not step over the ancient bounds or pass beyond the divine tradition. . . .

Chapter 8. Therefore, we believe in one God: one principle, without beginning, uncreated, unbegotten, indestructible and immortal, eternal, unlimited, uncircumscribed, unbounded, infinite in power, simple, uncompounded, incorporeal, unchanging, unaffected, unchangeable, inalterate, invisible, source of goodness and justice, light intellectual and inaccessible; power which no measure can give any idea of but which is measured only by His own will, for He can do all things whatsoever He pleases; maker of all things both visible and invisible, holding together all things and conserving them, provider for all, governing and dominating and ruling over all in unending and immortal reign; without contradiction, filling all things, contained by nothing, but Himself containing all things, being their conserver and first possessor; pervading all substances without being defiled, removed far beyond all things and every substance as being supersubstantial and surpassing all, supereminently divine and good and replete; appointing all the principalities and orders, set above every principality and order, above essence and life and speech and concept; light itself and goodness and being in so far as having neither being nor anything else that is from any other; the very source of being for all things that are, of life to the living, of speech to the articulate, and the cause of all good things for all; knowing all things before they begin to be; one substance, one godhead, one virtue, one will, one operation, one principality, one power, one domination, one kingdom; known in three perfect Persons and adored with one adoration, believed in and worshiped by every rational creature, united without confusion and distinct without separation, which is beyond understanding. We believe in Father and Son and Holy Ghost in whom we have been baptized. For it is thus that the Lord enjoined the Apostles: "Baptizing them in the name of the Father and of the Son and of the Holy Ghost."

We believe in one Father, the principle and cause of all things, begotten of no one, who alone is uncaused and unbegotten, the maker of all things and by nature Father of His one and only-begotten Son, our Lord and God and Savior, Jesus Christ, and Emitter of the All-Holy Spirit. We also believe in one Son of God, the only-begotten, our Lord Jesus Christ, who was begotten of the Father before all the ages, light from light, true God from true God, begotten not made, consubstantial with the Father, by whom all things were made; in regard to whom, when we say that He is before all ages, we mean that His begetting is outside of time and without beginning, for the Son of God was not brought from nothing into being; who is the brightness of the glory and the figure of the substance of the Father, His living power and wisdom, the subsistent Word, the substantial and perfect and living image of the invisible God. Actually, He was always with the Father, being begotten of Him eternally and without beginning. For the Father never was when the Son was not, but the Father and the Son begotten of Him exist together simultaneously, because the Father could not be so called without a Son. Now, if He was not Father when He did not have the Son, and then later became Father without having been Father before, then He was changed from not being Father to being Father, which is the worst of all blasphemies. For it is impossible to speak of God as naturally lacking the power of begetting. And the power of begetting is the power to beget of oneself, that is, of one's own substance, offspring similar to oneself in nature.

Accordingly, it is impious to say that time intervened in the begetting of the Son and that the Son came into existence after the Father. For we say that the begetting of the Son is of the Father, that is to say, of His nature; and if we do not grant that the Son begotten of the Father exists together with Him from the beginning, then we are introducing a change into the substance of the Father: namely, that He once was not Father, but became Father later. Now, creation, even if it was made at a later time, was not of the substance of God, but was brought from nothing into being by His will and power and does not involve any change in the nature of God. Begetting means producing of the substance of the begetter an offspring similar in substance to the begetter. Creation, on the other hand—making—is the bringing into being from the outside and not from the substance of the creator, of something created and made entirely dissimilar [in substance]. . . .

We likewise believe in the Holy Ghost, the Lord and Giver of life, who proceeds from the Father and abides in the Son; who is adored and glorified together with the Father and the Son as consubstantial and co-eternal with Them; who is the true and authoritative Spirit of God and the source of wisdom and life and sanctification; who is God together with the Father and the Son and is so proclaimed; who is uncreated, complete, creative, almighty, all-working, all-powerful, infinite in power; who dominates all creation but is not dominated; who deifies but is not deified; who fills but is not filled; who is shared in but does not share; who sanctifies but is not sanctified; who, as receiving the intercessions of all, is the Intercessor; who is like the Father and the Son in all things; who proceeds from the Father and is communicated through the Son and is participated in by all creation; who through Himself creates and gives substance to all things and sanctifies and preserves them; who is distinctly subsistent and exists in His own Person indivisible and inseparable from the Father and the Son; who has all things whatsoever the Father and the Son have except the being unbegotten and the being begotten. For the Father is uncaused and unbegotten, because He is not from anything, but has His being from Himself and does not have from any other anything whatsoever that He has. Rather, He Himself is the principle and cause by which all things naturally exist as they do. And the Son is begotten of the Father, while the Holy Ghost is Himself also of the Father—although not by begetting, but by procession. Now, we have learned that there is a difference between begetting and procession, but what the manner of this difference is we have not learned at all. However, the begetting of the Son and the procession of the Holy Ghost from the Father are simultaneous. . . .

Book 3

Chapter 13. Since we confess our Lord Jesus Christ to be at once both perfect God and perfect man, we declare that this same One has all things that the Father has, except the being unbegotten, and, with the sole exception of sin, all that the first Adam has; namely, a body and a rational and intellectual soul. We furthermore declare that corresponding to His two natures He has the twofold set of natural properties belonging to the two natures—two natural wills, the divine and the human; two natural operations, a divine and a human; two natural freedoms, a divine and a human; and wisdom and knowledge, both divine and human. For, since He is consubstantial with God the Father, He freely wills and acts as God. And, since He is also consubstantial with us, the same one freely wills and acts as man. Thus, the miracles are His, and so are the sufferings.

Chapter 14. Since, then, Christ has two natures, we say that He has two natural wills and two natural operations. On the other hand, since these two natures have one Person, we say that He is one and the same who wills and acts naturally according to both natures, of which and in which is Christ our God, and which are Christ our God. And we say that He wills and acts in each, not independently, but in concert. "For in each form He wills and acts in communion with the other." For the will and operation of things having the same substance is the same, and the will and operation of things having different substances is different. Conversely, the substance of things having the same will and operation is the same, whereas that of things having a different will and operation is different.

Thus, in Father and Son and Holy Ghost we discover the identity of nature from the identity of the operation and the will. In the divine incarnation, on the other hand, we discover the difference of the nature from the difference of the wills and operations, and knowing the difference of the natures we confess the difference of the wills and operations. For, just as the number of the natures piously understood and declared to belong to one and the same Christ does not divide this one Christ, but shows that the difference of the natures is maintained even in the union, neither does the number of the wills and operations belonging substantially to His natures introduce any division—God forbid—for in both of His natures He wills and acts for our salvation. On the contrary, their number shows the preservation and maintenance of the natures even in the union, and this alone. We do not call the wills and operations personal, but natural. I am referring to that very faculty of willing and acting by force of which things which will will and things which act act. For, if we concede these to be personal, then we shall be forced to say that the three Persons of the Holy Trinity differ in will and operation.

From *Saint John of Damascus: Writings,* translated by Frederic H. Chase, Jr. (The Fathers of the Church), pages 165–166, 176–179, 183–184, 295–297. Copyright 1958 by Fathers of the Church, Inc. Used by permission of The Catholic University of America Press.

Theodore the Studite (759–826)

From *First Refutation of the Iconoclasts*

Theodore, like John of Damascus, was a court official who became a monk, but since he had been an official at a Christian court, he found himself much more embroiled in theological disputes with the emperor. Emperor Leo the Isaurian (ruled 717–741) and his son Constantine V (741–775) had attempted to impose iconoclasm, the destruction of icons, on the empire, on the grounds that such images were idols. John of Damascus began the attack against iconoclasm; this is a section from Theodore's classic refutation of the iconoclasts a century later. Christological arguments proved crucial to his case.

2. The heretics say, "Surely there is not just one veneration, if our piety is shown to have many objects of veneration by the erection of icons, a practice which by some wile of the devil has been transferred from pagan tradition, bringing the veneration of idols into the catholic church. For every theologian agrees that the Godhead is entirely incomprehensible and uncircumscribable." . . .

We, however, have only one God whom we venerate as Trinity. And in regard to the doctrine of theology, so far from inventing some kind of circumscription or comprehension (perish the idea! for this was an invention of pagan thought), we do not even know that the Godhead exists at all, or what sort of thing it is, as it alone understands about itself. But because of his great goodness one of the Trinity has entered human nature and become like us. There is a mixture of the immiscible, a compound of the uncombinable: that is, of the uncircumscribable with the circumscribed, of the boundless with the bounded, of the limitless with the limited, of the formless with the well-formed (which is indeed paradoxical). For this reason Christ is depicted in images, and the invisible is seen. He who in His own divinity is uncircumscribable accepts the circumscription natural to His body. Both natures are revealed by the facts for what they are: otherwise one or the other nature would falsify what it is, as your opinions imply. . . .

3. . . . Neither one makes the other into something new, nor departs from what it was itself; nor is one changed into the other (for such a change would produce the confusion which we have refused to admit); but He is one and the same in His hypostasis, with His two natures unconfused in their proper spheres. Therefore you must either accept the "circumscribed," or if not, then take away the "visible" and "tangible" and "graspable" and whatever adjectives are in the same category. Then it would become obvious that you utterly deny that the Word became flesh—which is the height of impiety. . . .

5. "The erection of images is completely forbidden," the heretics say, "in the Scripture; for it says, 'You shall not make an idol for yourself, nor any likeness of whatever is in the heaven above or on the earth or in the waters under the earth. You shall not venerate them, nor shall you worship them, for I am the Lord your God.' "

When and to whom were these words spoken? Before the age of grace, and to those who "were confined under the Law," and were being taught the monarchy of one divine person; when God had not yet been revealed in the flesh, and the men of antiquity were being protected against foreign idols. This law had to be made for those who through their forefather Abraham had formed a chosen people and fled the abyss of polytheism, because there is one God and Lord of all, "whom no man has ever seen or can see," as it is written. For Him there is no designation, no likeness, no circumscription, no definition, nothing at all of what comes within the comprehension of the human mind. . . .

7. "It is a degradation," the heretics say, "and a humiliation, to depict Christ in material representations. It is better that He should remain in mental contemplation, as He is formed in us by the Holy Spirit, who sends into us a kind of divine formation through sanctification and righteousness." . . .

You cannot seem to avoid repeating yourself like a blind man going in circles, as you keep maliciously shifting from one thing to another. The very thing which you call indecent and abject is actually godlike and sublime because of the greatness of the mystery. For is it not glorious for the lofty when they humble themselves, as it is shameful for the lowly when they exalt themselves? Thus for Christ, who remains on His own summit of divinity, glorified in His immaterial indescribability, it is glory to be materially circumscribed in His own body because of His sublime condescension toward us.

Patriarch Photius of Constantinople (c.810–c.895)

From *Encyclical Letter to the Archiepiscopal Sees of the East*

As Patriarch of Constantinople, Photius was leader of the Eastern church, and he set out the fundamental differences it had with the West, as he made the first formal break. The immediate occasion of the quarrel concerned whether the newly converted Bulgarians would be part of the sphere of influence of Constantinople or Rome.

Encyclical letter to the archiepiscopal sees of the East, that is, Alexandria and the rest, in which the solutions of certain doubtful conclusions are considered, and that it is not permissible to say that the Holy Spirit proceeds from the Father and the Son, but from the Father alone. . . .

Now the barbarian tribe of the Bulgarians, who were hostile and inimical to Christ, has been converted to a surprising degree of meekness and knowledge of God. Beyond all expectation they have in a body embraced the faith of Christ, departing from the worship of devils and of their ancestral gods, and rejecting the error of pagan superstition.

But what a wicked and malignant design, what an ungodly state of affairs! Here is the story: The previous assumption of good news has been turned into dejection, delight and joy are changed into sadness and tears. That people had not embraced the true religion of Christians for even two years when certain impious and ominous men (or by whatever name a Christian refers to them) emerged from the darkness (for they have risen up out of the West)—Oh, how will I go on to tell the rest?—These, as I have said, in a tribe so recently established in piety, which joined the Church just a short time ago, as lightning or an earthquake or a heavy hail—actually I should say, like a wild boar greedily leaping into the much loved and newly planted vineyard of the Lord with feet and bared teeth—on paths of dishonorable administration and corrupted doctrine, thus boldly dividing up the country for themselves, have brought ruin on the people. They have villainously devised to lead them away from the true and pure doctrine and from an unblemished Christian faith and in this way destroy them.

The first unlawful practice they have set up is fasting on Saturday. Such slight disregard for the traditional teaching usually leads to the complete abandonment of the entire doctrine.

They separated the first week of Lent from the rest and allowed them milk, cheese and other gluttonous practices during this time. From here they made the road of transgressions wider and wider and removed the people more and more from the straight and royal road.

They taught them to despise the priest living in lawful matrimony and by rejecting matrimony spread the seed of Manichaeism, while they themselves practiced adultery. . . .

They have not only introduced the committing of such outrages, but now the crown of all evils is sprung up. Besides these offences that have already been mentioned, they have attempted to adulterate the sacred and holy creed, which has been approved by the vote of all the ecumenical synods and has unconquerable strength, with spurious arguments, interpolated words, and rash exaggerations. They are preaching a novel doctrine: that the Holy Spirit proceeds not from the Father alone, but from the Son as well.

Translated by the Monks of St. John's Abbey. From *Readings in Church History,* edited by Colman J. Barry, revised edition (Westminster, Md.: Christian Classics, 1985), pages 314–315. Copyright © 1985 by Colman J. Barry. Used by permission of the editor.

Pope Nicholas I (c.819–867)

From *Letter to Archbishop Hincmar of Reims and the Bishops of the Western Empire*

Nicholas was Pope from 858 to 867. He replied to Photius' condemnation by condemning Photius in turn, and this letter looks at some of the same issues from the other side.

. . . Inflamed with hate and envy against us, as we will specify later, they attempt to accuse us of heresy. With hatred indeed, for we not only disapproved but even condemned by deposition and anathematization the advancement attained by Photius, a neophyte, usurper, and adulterer of the Church of Constantinople. . . .

Instead they wish, rather, eagerly try to lead the Bulgarians from obedience to blessed Peter and to subject them shrewdly to their own authority under the pretext of the Christian religion. . . .

They strive particularly to find fault with our church and generally with every church which speaks Latin, because we fast on Saturdays and profess that the Holy Spirit proceeds from the Father and the Son, whereas they confess that He proceeds merely from the Father. Besides this, they claim that we detest marriage, since we do not allow priests to marry. . . .

As regards the procession of the Holy Spirit—who does not know that distinguished men, especially among the Latins, have written much about this matter? Supported by their authority we can reply fully and reasonably to their senselessness. Does any custom demand that they should go unrefuted, or that we should not answer their yelps and disputatious tongues with reasonable argument?

Is it even strange that they should allege such things since they even glory in the assertion that when the emperors moved from Rome to Constantinople the primacy of the Roman See also went to

Constantinople, and with the royal dignities even the privileges of the Roman Church were transferred? So that this same Photius, a usurper in the Church, even entitles himself in his writings, "archbishop and universal patriarch."

Translated by the Monks of St. John's Abbey. From *Readings in .Church History,* edited by Colman J. Barry, revised edition (Westminster, Md.: Christian Classics, 1985), pages 316–317, 319. Copyright © 1985 by Colman J. Barry. Used by permission of the editor.

Symeon the New Theologian (949–1022)

From *The Discourses*

Symeon, a monk on Mount Athos, was the first great exponent of hesychasm. The hesychasts practiced special forms of prayer and meditation and claimed a vision of the "uncreated light," which the apostles had seen surround Christ on Mount Tabor at the Transfiguration.

Chapter 15. 3. Let no one deceive you! God is light [1 John 1:15], and to those who have entered into union with Him He imparts of His own brightness to the extent that they have been purified. When the lamp of the soul, that is, the mind, has been kindled, then it knows that a divine fire has taken hold of it and inflamed it. How great a marvel! Man is united to God spiritually and physically, since the soul is not separated from the mind, neither the body from the soul. By being united in essence man also has three hypostases by grace. He is a single god by adoption with body and soul and the divine Spirit, of whom he has become a partaker. Then is fulfilled what was spoken by the prophet David, "I have said, ye are gods, and ye are all the sons of the Most High" [Ps. 82:6], that is, sons of the Most High according to the image of the Most High and according to His likeness [Gen. 1:26]. We become the divine offspring of the Divine Spirit [John 3:8], to whom the Lord rightly said and continues to say, "Abide in Me, that you may bring forth much fruit" [John 15:4, 8]. . . . It is evident that just as the Father abides in His own Son [John 14:10] and the Son in His Father's bosom [John 1:18] by nature, so those who have been born anew through the divine Spirit [John 3:3, 5] and by His gift have become the brothers of Christ our God and sons of God and gods by adoption, by grace abide in God and God in them [1 John 4:12ff.]. . . .

Chapter 16. 1. Brethren and fathers and children, A young man has told me this story:

3. ". . . Once I was so greatly moved to tears and loving desire for God that I would be unable to describe in words the joy and delight I then felt. I fell prostrate on the ground, and at once I saw, and behold, a great light was immaterially shining on me and seized hold of my whole mind and soul, so that I was struck with amazement at the unexpected marvel and I was, as it were, in ecstasy. Moreover, I forgot the place where I stood, who I was, and where, and could only cry out, 'Lord, have mercy,' so that when I came to myself I discovered that I was reciting this. But Father," said he, "who it was that was speaking and who moved my tongue, I do not know—only God knows. 'Whether I was in the body, or outside the body' [2 Cor. 12:2, 3], I conversed with this Light. The Light itself knows it; it scattered whatever mist there was in my soul and cast out every earthly care. It expelled from me all material denseness and bodily heaviness that made my members to be sluggish and numb. What an awesome marvel! It so invigorated and strengthened my limbs and muscles, which had been faint through great weariness, that it seemed to me as though I was stripping myself of the garment of corruption. Besides, there was poured into my soul in unutterable fashion a great spiritual joy and perception and a sweetness surpassing every taste of visible objects, together with a freedom and forgetfulness of all thoughts pertaining to this life. In a marvelous way there was granted to me and revealed to me the manner of the departure from this present life. Thus all the perceptions of my mind and my soul were wholly concentrated on the ineffable joy of that Light." . . .

5. ". . . The light envelops me and appears to me like a star, and is incomprehensible to all. It is radiant like the sun, and I perceive all creation encompassed by it. It shows me all that it contains, and enjoins me to respect my own limits. I am hemmed in by roof and walls, yet it opens the heavens to me. I lift up my eyes sensibly to contemplate the things that are on high, and I see all things as they were before. I marvel at what has happened, and I hear a voice speaking to me secretly from on high, 'These things are but symbols and preliminaries, for you will not see that which is perfect as long as you are clothed in flesh. But return to yourself and see that you do nothing that deprives you of the things that are above. Should you fall, however, it is to recall you to humility! Do not cease to cultivate

penitence, for when it is united to My love for mankind it blots out past and present failures.' "

Gregory Palamas (c.1296–1359)

From *The Triads*

Gregory grew up as a ward of the emperor but in the now familiar pattern left the court to become a monk. He modified the extreme claims of hesychasm while generally defending it. He explained the "uncreated light" as one of the "energies" of God, which pour forth eternally from God and are therefore neither part of God's unknowable essence nor part of the creation that is separate from God but have a special status between the two. Gregory's theology brings together many of the themes of the Eastern tradition.

The human mind also, and not only the angelic, transcends itself, and by victory over the passions acquires an angelic form. It, too, will attain to that light and will become worthy of a supernatural vision of God, not seeing the divine essence, but seeing God by a revelation appropriate and analogous to Him. One sees, not in a negative way— for one does see something—but in a manner superior to negation. For God is not only beyond knowledge, but also beyond unknowing; His revelation itself is also truly a mystery of a most divine and an extraordinary kind, since the divine manifestations, even if symbolic, remain unknowable by reason of their transcendence. They appear, in fact, according to a law which is not appropriate to either human or divine nature—being, as it were, for us yet beyond us—so that no name can properly describe them. . . .

So, when the saints contemplate this divine light within themselves, seeing it by the divinizing communion of the Spirit, through the mysterious visitation of perfecting illuminations—then they behold the garment of their deification, their mind being glorified and filled by the grace of the Word, beautiful beyond measure in His splendor; just as the divinity of the Word on the mountain glorified with divine light the body conjoined to it. For "the glory which the Father gave Him," He Himself has given to those obedient to Him, as the Gospel says, and "He willed that they should be with Him and contemplate His glory."

How can this be accomplished corporeally, now that He Himself is no longer corporeally present after His ascension to the heavens? It is necessarily carried out in a spiritual fashion, for the mind becomes supercelestial, and as it were the companion of Him who passed beyond the heavens for our sake, since it is manifestly yet mysteriously united to God, and contemplates supernatural and ineffable visions, being filled with all the immaterial knowledge of a higher light. Then it is no longer the sacred symbols accessible to the senses that it contemplates, nor yet the variety of Sacred Scripture that it knows; it is made beautiful by the creative and primordial Beauty, and illumined by the radiance of God.

In the same way, according to the revealer and interpreter of their hierarchy, the ranks of supracosmic spirits above are hierarchically filled, in a way analogous to themselves, not only with the first-given knowledge and understanding, but with the first light in respect of the sublimest triadic initiation. Not only do they [the angels] participate in, and contemplate, the glory of the Trinity, but they likewise behold the manifestation of the light of Jesus, revealed to His disciples on Thabor. Judged worthy of this vision, they are initiated into Him, for He is Himself deifying light: They truly draw near to Him, and enjoy direct participation in His divinizing rays. . . .

The monks know that the essence of God transcends the fact of being inaccessible to the senses, since God is not only above all created things, but is even beyond Godhead. The excellence of Him Who surpasses all things is not only beyond all affirmation, but also beyond all negation; it exceeds all excellence that is attainable by the mind. This hypostatic light, seen spiritually by the saints, they know by experience to exist, as they tell us, and to exist not symbolically only, as do manifestations produced by fortuitous events; but it is an illumination immaterial and divine, a grace invisibly seen and ignorantly known. *What* it is, they do not pretend to know. . . .

This light is not the essence of God, for that is inaccessible and incommunicable; it is not an angel, for it bears the marks of the Master. Sometimes it makes a man go out from the body or else, without separating him from the body, it elevates him to an ineffable height. At other times, it transforms the body, and communicates its own splendor to it when, miraculously, the light which deifies the body becomes accessible to the bodily eyes. . . .

Since the Reality which transcends every intellectual power is impossible to comprehend, it is beyond all beings; such union with God is thus beyond all knowledge, even if it be called "knowledge" metaphorically, nor is it intelligible, even if it be called so. For how can what is beyond all intellect be called intelligible? In respect to its transcendence, it might better be called ignorance than knowledge. It cannot be a part or aspect of knowledge, just as the Superessential is not an aspect of the essential. Knowledge as a whole could not contain it, nor could this knowledge, when subdivided, possess it as one of its parts.

It can in fact be possessed by a kind of ignorance rather than knowledge. For by reason of its transcendence, it is also ignorance, or rather it is beyond ignorance. This union, then, is a unique reality. For whatever name one gives to it—union, vision, sense perception, knowledge, intellection, illumination—would not, properly speaking, apply to it, or else would properly apply to it alone. . . .

I should like to ask this man why he claims that only the divine essence is without beginning, whereas everything apart from it is of a created nature, and whether or not he thinks this essence is all-powerful. That is to say, does it possess the faculties of knowing, of prescience, of creating, of embracing all things in itself; does it possess providence, the power of deification and, in a word, all such faculties, or not? For if it does not have them, this essence is not God, even though it alone is unoriginate. If it does possess these powers, but acquired them subsequently, then there was a time when it was imperfect, in other words, was not God. However, if it possessed these faculties from eternity, it follows that not only is the divine essence unoriginate, but that each of its powers is also.

Nonetheless, there is only one unoriginate essence, the essence of God; none of the powers that inhere in it is an essence, so that all necessarily and always are *in* the divine essence. To use an obscure image, they exist in the divine essence as do the powers of the senses in what is called the common spiritual sense of the soul. Here is the manifest, sure and recognised teaching of the Church!

For just as there is only one single essence without beginning, the essence of God, and the essences other than it are seen to be of a created nature, and come to be through this sole unoriginate essence, the unique maker of essences—in the same way, there is only one single providential power without beginning, namely that of God,

whereas all other powers apart from it are of a created nature; and
it is the same with all the other natural powers of God. It is thus not
true that the essence of God is the only unoriginate reality, and that
all realities other than it are of a created nature.

My discourse (guided by the absolute and eternally preexisting
nature) now leads me briefly to show the unbelieving that not only
the divine powers (which the Fathers often call "natural energies"),
but also some works of God are without beginning, as the Fathers
also rightly affirm. For was it not needful for the work of providence
to exist before Creation, so as to cause each of the created things to
come to be in time, out of nonbeing? Was it not necessary for a divine
knowledge to know before choosing, even outside time? But how
does it follow that the divine prescience had a beginning? How could
one conceive of a beginning of God's self-contemplation, and was
there ever a moment when God began to be moved toward contemplation of Himself? Never!

There is, therefore, a single unoriginate providence, that of God,
and it is a work of God. Providences other than it are of a created
nature. Nonetheless, providence is not the divine essence, and thus
the essence of God is not alone unoriginate. There is in the same way
only one unoriginate and uncreated prescience, that of God, whereas
presciences different from it—those which we possess by nature—all
have a beginning and are created. There is also only one will without
beginning, that of God, whereas all wills other than it have a beginning. However, no one would dare to say that the essence of God is
a will, not even those who claimed the Word of God was a son of
God's will. As for predeterminations, their very name shows that
they existed before creation; and should anyone wish to deny their
existence before the ages, he would be refuted by Paul's words, that
"God has foreordained before the ages."

These works of God, then, are manifestly unoriginate and pre-
temporal: His foreknowledge, will, providence, contemplation of
Himself, and whatever powers are akin to these. But if this
contemplation, providence, prescience, predetermination and will
are works of God that are without beginning, then virtue is also
unoriginate, for each of His works is a virtue; existence is also
unoriginate, since it precedes not only essence but all beings, for
it is the first existence. And are not will and predetermination
virtues? . . .

Thus neither the uncreated goodness, nor the eternal glory, nor the
divine life nor things akin to these *are* simply the superessential

essence of God, for God transcends them all as Cause. But we say He is life, goodness and so forth, and give Him these names, because of the revelatory energies and powers of the Superessential. As Basil the Great says, "The guarantee of the existence of every essence is its natural energy which leads the mind to the nature." And according to St. Gregory of Nyssa and all the other Fathers, the natural energy is the power which manifests every essence, and only nonbeing is deprived of this power; for the being which participates in an essence will also surely participate in the power which naturally manifests that essence.

CHAPTER 5

Augustine

In any history of Christian theology, Augustine (354–430) deserves a chapter to himself. Other than the Bible itself, he was the most honored authority throughout medieval theology, and the Reformation has with some justice been described as a debate between a Protestant emphasis on Augustine's doctrine of grace and a Catholic emphasis on his doctrine of the church.

Though his mother was a devout Christian, he turned away from the church in his youth. For a while he followed Manicheanism, a group founded in Babylonia and Persia in the 200s. The Manicheans believed the world to be a battleground between two divine forces, one good and one evil, in which our own actions are determined by powers beyond our control. Augustine gradually came to feel that that freed us too easily from responsibility for the evil we do. He turned to Platonism, which always remained a dominant intellectual influence on him but somehow lacked the moral force to change his life. For that, in the end, he came back to the Christian church, eventually becoming a bishop of the North African city of Hippo and entering into all the theological controversies of his time.

One such controversy concerned Donatism. In the last great persecution of Christians, some North African bishops had turned Bibles over to the Roman authorities to avoid torture and death. The Donatist party argued that ordinations and baptisms performed by such corrupt church officials were invalid, and the issue bitterly divided North African Christians. Augustine led the fight against the Donatists and even sought imperial support in suppressing them.

Another conflict, this one with the Pelagians, arose in part from Augustine's own work. In his *Confessions* he had maintained that he had been totally unable to move toward salvation by his own efforts and had been rescued only by God's grace. The British monk Pelagius (c.360–c.431) thought that such an emphasis discouraged Christians from seeking moral improvement in their lives and that it takes our efforts to earn God's help. In response to Pelagius, Augustine insisted that God's election of some to salvation cannot be earned but comes only through unmerited grace.

In Augustine's later years the city of Rome fell to barbarian invaders, and some Roman pagans argued that the cause was the abandonment of the old gods. In his last great work, *The City of God,* Augustine offered a theology of history, refuting the ultimacy of Rome's claims and tracing through all time the stories of the city of men and the city of God.

Augustine

From *The Confessions*

When Augustine was sixteen, his father ran short of money, and he had to drop out of school and live at home for a year. He fell into bad company. About thirty years later, in 401, as a Christian bishop writing his autobiographical Confessions, *he looked back on his youthful indiscretions. The Platonic philosophy, which so influenced him, taught that we sin only out of ignorance. If we really recognize that something is wrong, we will not do it. From his own experience Augustine concluded otherwise.*

Book 2

Chapter 4. 9. . . . There was a pear tree close to our own vineyard, heavily laden with fruit, which was not tempting either for its color or for its flavor. Late one night—having prolonged our games in the streets until then, as our bad habit was—a group of young scoundrels, and I among them, went to shake and rob this tree. We carried off a huge load of pears, not to eat ourselves, but to dump out to the hogs, after barely tasting some of them ourselves. Doing this pleased us all the more because it was forbidden. Such was my heart, O God, such was my heart—which thou didst pity even in that bottomless pit. Behold, now let my heart confess to thee what it was seeking there, when I was being gratuitously wanton, having no inducement to evil but the evil itself. It was foul, and I loved it. I loved my own undoing. I loved my error—not that for which I erred but the error itself. A depraved soul, falling away from security in thee to destruction in itself, seeking nothing from the shameful deed but shame itself. . . .

Chapter 6. 12. What was it in you, O theft of mine, that I, poor wretch, doted on—you deed of darkness—in that sixteenth year of my age? Beautiful you were not, for you were a theft. But are you anything at all, so that I could analyze the case with you? Those pears that we stole were fair to the sight because they were thy creation, O Beauty beyond compare, O Creator of all, O thou good God—God the highest good and my true good. Those pears were truly pleasant to the sight, but it was not for them that my miserable soul lusted, for I had an abundance of better pears. I stole those simply that I might steal, for, having stolen them, I threw them away. My sole gratification in them was my own sin, which I was pleased to enjoy; for, if any one of these pears entered my mouth, the only good flavor it had was my sin in eating it. And now, O Lord my God, I ask what it was in that theft of mine that caused me such delight; for behold it had not beauty of its own—certainly not the sort of beauty that exists in justice and wisdom, nor such as is in the mind, memory, senses, and the animal life of man; nor yet the kind that is the glory and beauty of the stars in their courses; nor the beauty of the earth, or the sea—teeming with spawning life, replacing in birth that which dies and decays. Indeed, it did not have that false and shadowy beauty which attends the deceptions of vice. . . .

Chapter 9. 17. By what passion, then, was I animated? It was undoubtedly depraved and a great misfortune for me to feel it. But still, what was it? "Who can understand his errors?" [Ps. 19:12].

We laughed because our hearts were tickled at the thought of deceiving the owners, who had no idea of what we were doing and would have strenuously objected. Yet, again, why did I find such delight in doing this which I would not have done alone? Is it that no one readily laughs alone? No one does so readily, but still sometimes, when men are by themselves and no one else is about, a fit of laughter will overcome them when something very droll presents itself to their sense or mind. Yet alone I would not have done it—alone I could not have done it at all.

Behold, my God, the lively review of my soul's career is laid bare before thee. I would not have committed that theft alone. My pleasure in it was not what I stole but, rather, the act of stealing. Nor would I have enjoyed doing it alone—indeed I would not have done it! O friendship all unfriendly! You strange seducer of the soul, who hungers for mischief from impulses of mirth and wantonness, who craves another's loss without any desire for one's own profit or revenge—so that, when they say, "Let's go, let's do it," we are ashamed not to be shameless.

Chapter 10. 18. Who can unravel such a twisted and tangled knottiness? It is unclean. I hate to reflect upon it. I hate to look on it. But I do long for thee, O Righteousness and Innocence, so beautiful and comely to all virtuous eyes—I long for thee with an insatiable satiety. With thee is perfect rest, and life unchanging. He who enters into thee enters into the joy of his Lord, and shall have no fear and shall achieve excellence in the Excellent. I fell away from thee, O my God, and in my youth I wandered too far from thee, my true support. And I became to myself a wasteland.

Book 3

Chapter 1. 1. I came to Carthage, where a caldron of unholy loves was seething and bubbling all around me. I was not in love as yet, but I was in love with love; and, from a hidden hunger, I hated myself for not feeling more intensely a sense of hunger. I was looking for something to love, for I was in love with loving, and I hated security and a smooth way, free from snares. Within me I had a dearth of that inner food which is thyself, my God—although that dearth caused me no hunger. And I remained without any appetite for incorruptible food—not because I was already filled with it, but because the emptier I became the more I loathed it. Because of this my soul was unhealthy; and, full of sores, it exuded itself forth, itching to be scratched by scraping on the things of the senses [Job 2:7, 8]. Yet, had these things no soul, they would certainly not inspire our love.

To love and be loved was sweet to me, and all the more when I gained the enjoyment of the body of the person I loved. Thus I polluted the spring of friendship with the filth of concupiscence and I dimmed its luster with the slime of lust. Yet, foul and unclean as I was, I still craved, in excessive vanity, to be thought elegant and urbane. And I did fall precipitately into the love I was longing for. My God, my mercy, with how much bitterness didst thou, out of thy infinite goodness, flavor that sweetness for me! For I was not only beloved but also I secretly reached the climax of enjoyment; and yet I was joyfully found with troublesome ties, so that I could be scourged with the burning iron rods of jealousy, suspicion, fear, anger, and strife.

Fifteen years after that trip to Carthage, with a mistress and an illegitimate son, Augustine was still struggling with his passions. He had moved to Rome and then to Milan, where he was deeply influenced by the preaching of its bishop, Ambrose. By this point he wanted to become a Christian, but full commitment came hard. On the crucial day he was sitting in a garden with his friend Alypius.

Book 8

Chapter 11. 25. Thus I was sick and tormented, reproaching myself more bitterly than ever, rolling and writhing in my chain till it should be utterly broken. By now I was held but slightly, but still was held. And thou, O Lord, didst press upon me in my inmost heart with a severe mercy, redoubling the lashes of fear and shame; lest I should again give way and that same slender remaining tie not be broken off, but recover strength and enchain me yet more securely.

I kept saying to myself, "See, let it be done now; let it be done now." And as I said this I all but came to a firm decision. I all but did it—yet I did not quite. Still I did not fall back to my old condition, but stood aside for a moment and drew breath. And I tried again, and lacked only a very little of reaching the resolve—and then somewhat less, and then all but touched and grasped it. Yet I still did not quite reach or touch or grasp the goal, because I hesitated to die to death and live to life. And the worse way, to which I was habituated, was stronger in me than the better, which I had not tried. And up to the very moment in which I was to become another man, the nearer the moment approached, the greater horror did it strike in me. But it did not strike me back, nor turn me aside, but held me in suspense. . . .

Chapter 12. 28. Now when deep reflection had drawn up out of the secret depths of my soul all my misery and had heaped it up before the sight of my heart, there arose a mighty storm, accompanied by a mighty rain of tears. That I might give way fully to my tears and lamentations, I stole away from Alypius, for it seemed to me that solitude was more appropriate for the business of weeping. I went far enough away that I could feel that even his presence was no restraint upon me. This was the way I felt at the time, and he realized it. I suppose I had said something before I started up and he noticed that the sound of my voice was choked with weeping. And so he stayed alone, where we had been sitting together, greatly astonished. I flung myself down under a fig tree—how I know not—and gave free course to my tears. The streams of my eyes gushed out an acceptable sacrifice to thee. And, not indeed in these words, but to this effect, I cried to thee: "And thou, O Lord, how long? How long, O Lord? Wilt thou be angry forever? Oh, remember not against us our former iniquities" [cf. Ps. 6:3; 79:8]. For I felt that I was still enthralled by them. I sent up these sorrowful cries: "How long, how long? Tomorrow and tomorrow? Why not now? Why not this very hour make an end to my uncleanness?"

29. I was saying these things and weeping in the most bitter contrition of my heart, when suddenly I heard the voice of a boy or a girl—I know not which—coming from the neighboring house, chanting over and over again, "Pick it up, read it; pick it up, read it." Immediately I ceased weeping and began most earnestly to think whether it was usual for children in some kind of game to sing such a song, but I could not remember ever having heard the like. So, damming the torrent of my tears, I got to my feet, for I could not but think that this was a divine command to open the Bible and read the first passage I should light upon. For I had heard how Anthony, accidentally coming into church while the gospel was being read, received the admonition as if what was read had been addressed to him: "Go and sell what you have and give it to the poor, and you shall have the treasure in heaven; and come and follow me" [Matt. 19:21]. By such an oracle he was forthwith converted to thee.

So I quickly returned to the bench where Alypius was sitting, for there I had put down the apostle's book when I had left there. I snatched it up, opened it, and in silence read the paragraph on which my eye first fell: "Not in rioting and drunkenness, not in chambering and wantonness, not in strife and envying, but put on the Lord Jesus Christ, and make no provision for the flesh to fulfill the lusts thereof" [Rom. 13:13]. I wanted to read no further, nor did I need to. For instantly, as the sentence ended, there was infused in my heart something like the light of full certainty and all the gloom of doubt vanished away.

From *Augustine: Confessions and Enchiridion,* translated and edited by Albert C. Outler (Volume VII: The Library of Christian Classics), pages 54–56, 59–62, 173–176. First published in MCMLV by SCM Press Ltd., London, and The Westminster Press, Philadelphia. Used by permission of the publishers.

Augustine

From *On Free Will*

*Augustine began this work around 387, two years after his conver-
sion, and returned to it and completed it about 395. Against the
Manicheans, whom he had earlier followed, he now argued that we are
responsible for our evil actions, for we choose them freely. The Manicheans explained evil as the product of a force independent of the good
God. Insisting on the omnipotence of God, Augustine had to explain
why God gives us freedom to do evil and how that freedom can be
compatible with God's foreknowledge of what we will do. He cast the
treatise in the form of a dialogue with his friend Evodius.*

Book II, 1

Evodius: Now explain to me, if it can be done, why God has given
man free choice in willing, for if he had not received that freedom
he would not have been able to sin.

Augustine: You hold it to be certainly known that it is God who
has given man this power which you think ought not to have been
given.

Ev: No one else could have done so, I think. For we derive our
origin from him, and from him we merit punishment or reward
according as we sin or act rightly.

Aug: Here is another thing I desire to know. Do you know this
quite distinctly, or do you merely believe it, without knowing it,
because you allow yourself to be influenced by authority?

Ev: Undoubtedly I was first brought to believe this on the ground
of authority. But what can be more true than to say that every good
thing is from God, that justice is entirely good, and that it is just that
sinners should be punished and well-doers rewarded. Hence it follows that it is by God that sinners are made unhappy and well-doers
happy.

Aug: I am not objecting; but I ask the question: how do you know
that we derive our origin from God? You have not explained this
though you have explained how we merit punishment or reward at
his hand.

Ev: If it is accepted that God punishes sins, as it must be if it is
true that all justice has its source in him, this alone would prove that
we derive our origin from him. No doubt it is the characteristic of

goodness to confer benefits on strangers, but it is not similarly the mark of justice to punish sins in those who are not under its immediate jurisdiction. Hence it is clear that we belong to him because he is not only most kind in conferring benefits upon us, but also most just in his punishments. Moreover, from the statement I made and you accepted, that every good thing comes from God, it can be known that man also comes from God. For man, in so far as he is man, is good because he can live aright if he chooses to do so.

Aug: Clearly if this is so, the problem you have posed is solved. If man is good, and if he would not be able to act rightly except by willing to do so, he ought to have free will because without it he would not be able to act rightly. Because he also sins through having free will, we are not to believe that God gave it to him for that purpose. It is, therefore, a sufficient reason why he ought to have been given it, that without it man could not live aright. That it was given for this purpose can be understood from this fact. If anyone uses his free will in order to sin, God punishes him. That would be unjust unless the will was free not only to live aright but also to sin. How could he be justly punished who uses his will for the purpose for which it was given? Now when God punishes a sinner what else do you suppose he will say to him than "Why did you not use your free will for the purpose for which I gave it to you, that is, in order to do right?" Justice is praised as a good thing because it condemns sins and honours righteous actions. How could that be done if man had not free will? An action would be neither sinful nor righteous unless it were done voluntarily. For the same reason both punishment and reward would be unjust, if man did not have free will. But in punishing and in rewarding there must have been justice since justice is one of the good things which come from God. God, therefore, must have given and ought to have given man free will. . . .

Book III, 2

_Ev:_ That being so, I have a deep desire to know how it can be that God knows all things beforehand and that, nevertheless, we do not sin by necessity. Whoever says that anything can happen otherwise than as God has foreknown it, is attempting to destroy the divine foreknowledge with the most insensate impiety. If God foreknew that the first man would sin—and that anyone must concede who acknowledges with me that God has foreknowledge of all future events—I do not say that God did not make him, for he made him good, nor that the sin of the creature whom he made good could be prejudicial to God. On the contrary, God showed his goodness in making man, his justice in punishing his sin, and his mercy in delivering him. I do not say, therefore, that God did not make man. But this I say. Since God foreknew that man would sin, that which God foreknew must necessarily come to pass. How then is the will free when there is apparently this unavoidable necessity? . . .

Book III, 3

Aug: Your trouble is this. You wonder how it can be that these two propositions are not contradictory and incompatible, namely that God has foreknowledge of all future events, and that we sin voluntarily and not by necessity. For if, you say, God foreknows that a man will sin, he must necessarily sin. But if there is necessity there is no voluntary choice in sinning, but rather fixed and unavoidable necessity. You are afraid that by that reasoning the conclusion may be reached either that God's foreknowledge of all future events must be impiously denied, or, if that cannot be denied, that sin is committed not voluntarily but by necessity. Isn't that your difficulty?

Ev: Exactly that.

Aug: You think, therefore, that all things of which God has foreknowledge happen by necessity and not voluntarily.

Ev: Yes. Absolutely.

Aug: Try an experiment, and examine yourself a little, and tell me what kind of will you are going to have to-morrow. Will you want to sin or to do right?

Ev: I do not know.

Aug: Do you think God also does not know?

Ev: I could in no wise think that.

Aug: If God knows what you are going to will to-morrow, and foresees what all men are going to will in the future, not only those who are at present alive but all who will ever be, much more will he foresee what he is going to do with the just and the impious?

Ev: Certainly if I say that God has foreknowledge of my deed, I should say with even greater confidence that he has foreknowledge of his own acts, and foresees with complete certainty what he is going to do.

Aug: Don't you see that you will have to be careful lest someone say to you that, if all things of which God has foreknowledge are done by necessity and not voluntarily, his own future acts will be done not voluntarily but by necessity?

Ev: When I said that all future events of which God has foreknowledge happen by necessity, I was having regard only to things which happen within his creation, and not to things which happen in God himself. Indeed, in God nothing happens. Everything is eternal.

Aug: God, then, is not active within his creation?

Ev: He determined once for all how the order of the universe he created was to go on, and he never changes his mind.

Aug: Does he never make anyone happy?

Ev: Indeed he does.

Aug: He does it precisely at the time when the man in question actually becomes happy.

Ev: That is so.

Aug: If, then, for example, you yourself are happy one year from now, you will be made happy at that time.

Ev: Exactly.

Aug: God knows to-day what he is going to do a year hence?

Ev: He eternally had that foreknowledge, but I agree that he has it now, if indeed it is to happen so.

Aug: Now tell me, are you not God's creature? And will not your becoming happy take place within your experience?

Ev: Certainly I am God's creature, and if I become happy it will be within my experience.

Aug: If God, then, makes you happy, your happiness will come by necessity and not by the exercise of your will?

Ev: God's will is my necessity.

Aug: Will you then be happy against your will?

Ev: If I had the power to be happy, I should be so at once. For I wish to be happy but am not, because not I but God makes me happy.

Aug: The truth simply cries out against you. You could not imagine that "having in our power" means anything else than "being able to do what we will." Therefore there is nothing so much in our power as is the will itself. For as soon as we will [*volumus*] immediately will [*voluntas*] is there. We can say rightly that we do not grow old voluntarily but necessarily, or that we do not die voluntarily but from necessity, and so with other similar things. But who but a raving fool would say that it is not voluntarily that we will? Therefore though God knows how we are going to will in the future, it is not proved that we do not voluntarily will anything. When you said that you did not make yourself happy, you said it as if I had denied it. What I say is that when you become happy in the future it will take place not against your will but in accordance with your willing. Therefore, though God has foreknowledge of your happiness in the future, and though nothing can happen otherwise than as he has foreknown it (for that would mean that there is no foreknowledge) we are not thereby compelled to think that you will not be happy voluntarily. That would be absurd and far from true. God's foreknowledge, which is even to-day quite certain that you are to be happy at a future date, does not rob you of your will to happiness when you actually attain happiness. Similarly if ever in the future you have a culpable will, it will be none the less your will because God had foreknowledge of it.

Observe, pray, how blind are those who say that if God has foreknowledge of what I am going to will, since nothing can happen otherwise than as he has foreknown it, therefore I must necessarily will what he has foreknown. If so, it must be admitted that I will, not voluntarily but from necessity. Strange folly! Is there, then, no difference between things that happen according to God's foreknowledge where there is no intervention of man's will at all, and things that happen because of a will of which he has foreknowledge? I omit the equally monstrous assertion of the man I mentioned a moment ago, who says I must necessarily so will. By assuming necessity he strives to do away with will altogether. If I must necessarily will, why need I speak of willing at all? But if he puts it in another way, and says that, because he must necessarily so will, his will is not in his own power, he can be countered by the answer you gave me when I asked whether you could become happy against your will. You replied that you would be happy now if the matter were in your power, for you willed to be happy but could not achieve it. And I added that the truth cries out against you; for we cannot say we do not have the power unless we do not have what we will. If we do not have the will, we may think we will but in fact we do not. If we cannot will without willing, those who will have will, and all that is in our power we have by willing. Our will would not be will unless it were in our power. Because it is in our power, it is free. We have nothing that is free which is not in our power, and if we have something it cannot be nothing. Hence it is not necessary to deny that God has foreknowledge of all things, while at the same time our wills are our own. God has foreknowledge of our will, so that of which he has foreknowledge must come to pass. In other words, we shall exercise our wills in the future because he has foreknowledge that we shall do so; and there can be no will or voluntary action unless it be in our power. Hence God has also foreknowledge of our power to will. My power is not taken from me by God's foreknowledge. Indeed I shall be more certainly in possession of my power because he whose foreknowledge is never mistaken, foreknows that I shall have the power.

Ev: Now I no longer deny that whatever God has foreknown must necessarily come to pass, nor that he has foreknowledge of our sins, but in such a way that our wills remain free and within our power.

From *Augustine: Earlier Writings,* edited and translated by John H. S. Burleigh (Volume VI: The Library of Christian Classics), pages 134–135, 172–176. First published in MCMLIII by SCM Press Ltd., London, and The Westminster Press, Philadelphia. Used by permission of the publishers.

Augustine

From *In Answer to the Letters of Petilian, the Donatist*

Petilian, a Donatist bishop, had written a letter to his followers defending the Donatist position: Baptisms performed by the Catholic party Augustine represented were often invalid, for they were performed by priests ordained by corrupt bishops who had betrayed the church in the time of persecution. Somewhere shortly after 400, Augustine responded in this treatise.

Chapter 1. 2. . . . Let us rather turn our attention to the mode in which he has sought to prove that we do not possess baptism, and that therefore they do not require the repetition of what was already present, but confer what hitherto was wanting. For he says, "What we look for is the conscience of the giver to cleanse that of the recipient." But supposing the conscience of the giver is concealed from view, and perhaps defiled with sin, how will it be able to cleanse the conscience of the recipient, if, as he says, "what we look for is the conscience of the giver to cleanse that of the recipient"? For if he should say that it makes no matter to the recipient what amount of evil may lie concealed from view in the conscience of the giver, perhaps that ignorance may have such a degree of efficacy as this, that a man cannot be defiled by the guilt of the conscience of him from whom he receives baptism, so long as he is unaware of it. Let it then be granted that the guilty conscience of his neighbor cannot defile a man so long as he is unaware of it, but is it therefore clear that it can further cleanse him from his own guilt?

Chapter 2. 3. Whence, then, is a man to be cleansed who receives baptism, when the conscience of the giver is polluted without the knowledge of him who is to receive it? Especially when he goes on to say, "For he who receives faith from the faithless receives not faith, but guilt." There stands before us one that is faithless ready to baptize, and he who should be baptized is ignorant of his faithlessness; what think you that he will receive? Faith, or guilt? If you answer faith, then you will grant that it is possible that a man should receive not guilt, but faith, from him that is faithless; and the former saying will be false, that "he who receives faith from the faithless receives not faith, but guilt." For we find that it is possible that a man should receive faith even from one that is faithless, if he be not aware of the faithlessness of the giver. For he does not say, He who receives faith from one that is openly and notoriously faithless; but he says, "He who receives faith from the faithless receives not faith, but guilt"; which certainly is false when a person is baptized by one who hides his faithlessness. But if he shall say, Even when the faithlessness of the baptizer is concealed, the recipient receives not faith from him, but guilt, then let them rebaptize those who are well known to have been baptized by men who in their own body have long concealed a life of guilt, but have eventually been detected, convicted, and condemned.

Chapter 3. For, so long as they escaped detection, they could not bestow faith on any whom they baptized, but only guilt, if it be true that whosoever receives faith from one that is faithless receives not faith, but guilt. Let them therefore be baptized by the good, that they may be enabled to receive not guilt, but faith.

4. But how, again, shall they have any certainty about the good who are to give them faith, if what we look to is the conscience of the giver, which is unseen by the eyes of the proposed recipient? Therefore, according to their judgment, the salvation of the spirit is made uncertain, so long as in opposition to the holy Scriptures, which say, "It is better to trust in the Lord than to put confidence in man" [Ps. 118:8], and "Cursed be the man that trusteth in man" [Jer. 17:5], they remove the hope of those who are to be baptized from the Lord their God, and persuade them that it should be placed

in man; the practical result of which is, that their salvation becomes not merely uncertain, but actually null and void. For "salvation belongeth unto the Lord" [Ps. 3:8], and "vain is the help of man" [Ps. 60:11]. Therefore, whosoever places his trust in man, even in one whom he knows to be just and innocent, is accursed. Whence also the Apostle Paul finds fault with those who said they were of Paul, saying, "Was Paul crucified for you? or were ye baptized in the name of Paul?" [1 Cor. 1:13].

Translated by J. R. King. From *Nicene and Post-Nicene Fathers,* 1st Series, edited by Philip Schaff (New York: Christian Literature Company, 1886–1890), Volume 4, pages 520–521.

Augustine

From *Concerning the Correction of the Donatists*

Conflict between the Donatist and Catholic parties had turned violent in North Africa, and Augustine and others had sought imperial help in forcing the Donatists into submission. The Donatists argued that the true church is that which is persecuted, not that which persecutes, and that force should not have been used against them. In this response, written in 417, Augustine begins by claiming that the Donatists, years earlier, had been the first to ask for imperial help, in their campaign against Caecilianus, the supposedly corrupt bishop of Carthage.

Chapter 2. 6. I would add, moreover, that they themselves, by making it the subject of an accusation, referred the case of Caecilianus to the decision of the Emperor Constantine; and that, even after the bishops had pronounced their judgment, finding that they could not crush Caecilianus, they brought him in person before the above-named emperor for trial, in the most determined spirit of persecution. And so they were themselves the first to do what they censure in us, in order that they may deceive the unlearned, saying that Christians ought not to demand any assistance from Christian emperors against the enemies of Christ. . . .

Chapter 5. 19. But as to the argument of those men who are unwilling that their impious deeds should be checked by the enactment of righteous laws, when they say that the apostles never sought such measures from the kings of the earth, they do not consider the different character of that age, and that everything comes in its own season. For what emperor had as yet believed in Christ, so as to serve Him in the cause of piety by enacting laws against impiety [in the time of the apostles]? . . .

20. Seeing, then, that the kings of the earth were not yet serving the Lord in the time of the apostles, but were still imagining vain things against the Lord and against His Anointed, that all might be fulfilled which was spoken by the prophets, it must be granted that at that time acts of impiety could not possibly be prevented by the laws, but were rather performed under their sanction. For the order of events was then so rolling on, that even the Jews were killing those who preached Christ, thinking that they did God service in so doing, just as Christ had foretold [John 16:2], and the heathen were raging against the Christians, and the patience of the martyrs was overcoming them all. But so soon as the fulfillment began of what it is written in a later psalm, "All kings shall fall down before Him; all nations shall serve Him" [Ps. 72:11], what sober-minded man could say to the kings, "Let not any thought trouble you within your kingdom as to who restrains or attacks the Church of your Lord; deem it not a matter in which you should be concerned, which of your subjects may choose to be religious or sacrilegious," seeing that you cannot say to them, "Deem it no concern of yours which of your subjects may choose to be chaste, or which unchaste"? For why, when free-will is given by God to man, should adulteries be punished by the laws, and sacrilege allowed? Is it a lighter matter that a soul should not keep faith with God, than that a woman should be faithless to her husband? Or if those faults which are committed not in contempt but in ignorance of religious truth are to be visited with lighter punishment, are they therefore to be neglected altogether?

Chapter 6. 21. It is indeed better (as no one ever could deny) that men should be led to worship God by teaching, than that they should be driven to it by fear of punishment or pain; but it does not follow that because the former course produces the better men, therefore those who do not yield to it should be neglected. For many have found advantage (as we have proved, and are daily proving by actual experiment), in being first compelled by fear or pain, so that they might afterwards be influenced by teaching, or might follow out in act what they had already learned in word. Some, indeed, set before us the sentiments of a certain secular author, who said,

> " 'Tis well, I ween, by shame the young to train,
> And dread of meanness, rather than by pain."

This is unquestionably true. But while those are better who are guided aright by love, those are certainly more numerous who are corrected by fear. For, to answer these persons out of their own author, we find him saying in another place,

> "Unless by pain and suffering thou art taught,
> Thou canst not guide thyself aright in aught."* . . .

23. Why, therefore, should not the Church use force in compelling her lost sons to return, if the lost sons compelled others to their destruction? Although even men who have not been compelled, but only led astray, are received by their loving mother with more affection if they are recalled to her bosom through the enforcement of terrible but salutary laws, and are the objects of far more deep congratulation than those whom she had never lost. Is it not a part of the care of the shepherd, when any sheep have left the flock, even though not violently forced away, but led astray by tender words and coaxing blandishments, to bring them back to the fold of his master when he has found them, by the fear, or even the pain of the whip?

Translated by J. R. King. From *Nicene and Post-Nicene Fathers,* 1st Series, edited by Philip Schaff (New York: Christian Literature Company, 1886–1890), Volume 4, pages 635, 640–642.

Augustine

From *On the Grace of Christ*

In 418 two Roman aristocrats Augustine had met earlier wrote him a letter reporting that Pelagius had modified his earlier views on grace and urging Augustine to seek a reconciliation. In reply, Augustine insisted that Pelagius was trying to mislead them and had not shifted on the central issues.

Chapter 4. In his system, [Pelagius] posits and distinguishes three faculties, by which he says God's commandments are fulfilled,— *capacity, volition,* and *action:* meaning by "capacity," that by which

---

*The first quotation comes from Terence's *The Brothers,* Act 1, Scene 1, lines 32–33; the second is not found in the extant plays of Terence.

a man is able to be righteous; by "volition" that by which he wills to be righteous; by "action," that by which he actually is righteous. The first of these, the capacity, he allows to have been bestowed on us by the Creator of our nature; it is not in our power, and we possess it even against our will. The other two, however, the volition and the action, he asserts to be our own; and he assigns them to us so strictly as to contend that they proceed simply from ourselves. In short, according to his view, God's grace has nothing to do with assisting those two faculties which he will have to be altogether our own, the volition and the action, but that only which is not in our own power and comes to us from God, namely the capacity; as if the faculties which are our own, that is, the volition and the action, have such avail for declining evil and doing good, that they require no divine help, whereas that faculty which we have of God, that is to say, the capacity, is so weak, that it is always assisted by the aid of grace. . . .

Chapter 6. . . . Whenever we read or hear of his acknowledging the assistance of divine grace in order to our avoidance of evil and accomplishment of good,—whatever he may mean by the said assistance of grace, whether law and the teaching or any other thing,—we are sure of what he says; nor can we run into any mistake by understanding him otherwise than he means. For we cannot help knowing that, according to his belief, it is not our "volition" nor our "action" which is assisted by the divine help, but solely our "capacity" to will and act, which alone of the three, as he affirms, we have of God. As if that faculty were infirm which God Himself placed in our nature; while the other two, which, as he would have it, are our own, are so strong and firm and self-sufficient as to require none of His help! so that He does not help us to will, nor help us to act, but simply helps us to the possibility of willing and acting.

The apostle, however, holds the contrary, when he says, "Work out your own salvation with fear and trembling" [Phil. 2:12]. And that they might be sure that it was not simply in their being able to work (for this they had already received in nature and in teaching), but in their actual working, that they were divinely assisted, the apostle does not say to them, "For it is God that worketh in you to be able," as if they already possessed volition and operation among their own resources, without requiring His assistance in respect of these two; but he says, "For it is God which worketh in you both to will and to perform of His own good pleasure" [Phil. 2:13]; or, as the reading runs in other copies, especially the Greek, "both to will and to operate." Consider, now, whether the apostle did not thus long before foresee by the Holy Ghost that there would arise adversaries of the grace of God; and did not therefore declare that God works within us those two very things, even "willing" and "operating," which this man so determined to be our own, as if they were in no wise assisted by the help of divine grace. . . .

Chapter 24. . . . Great indeed is the help of the grace of God, so that He turns our heart in whatever direction He pleases. But according to this writer's foolish opinion, however great the help may be, we deserve it all at the moment when, without any assistance beyond the liberty of our will, we hasten to the Lord, desire His guidance and direction, suspend our own will entirely on His, and by close adherence to Him become one spirit with Him. Now all these vast courses of goodness we (according to him) accomplish, forsooth, simply by the freedom of our own free will; and by reason of such antecedent merits we so secure His grace, that He turns our heart which way soever He pleases.

Well, now, how is *that* grace which is not gratuitously conferred? How can it be grace, if it is given in payment of a debt? How can that be true which the apostle says, "It is not of yourselves, but it is the gift of God; not of works, lest any man should boast" [Eph. 2:8, 9]; and again, "If it is of grace, then is it no more of works, otherwise grace is no more grace" [Rom. 11:6]: how, I repeat, can this be true, if such meritorious works precede as to procure for us the bestowal of grace? Surely, under the circumstances, there can be no gratuitous gift, but only the recompense of a due reward. Is it the case, then, that in order to find their way to the help of God, men run to God without God's help? And in order that we may receive God's help while cleaving to Him, do we without His help cleave to God? What greater gift, or even what similar gift, could grace itself bestow upon any man, if he has already without grace been able to make himself one spirit with the Lord by no other power than that of his own free will?

Translated by Peter Holmes. From *Nicene and Post-Nicene Fathers,* 1st Series, edited by Philip Schaff (New York: Christian Literature Company, 1886–1890), Volume 5, pages 218–219, 226.

Augustine

From *The City of God*

Alaric and his army of Goths sacked Rome in 410. Some of the refugees from Rome came to North Africa and argued that abandoning the pagan gods had led to Rome's fall. In The City of God, *begun in 413 and finished in 425, Augustine acknowledged the greatness of pagan Rome but maintained the limitations on it or any human power.*

Book 4

Chapter 3. Let us see how it is that they dare to ascribe the very great extent and duration of the Roman empire to those gods whom they contend that they worship honorably, even by the obsequies of vile games and the ministry of vile men: although I should like first to inquire for a little what reason, what prudence, there is in wishing to glory in the greatness and extent of the empire, when you cannot point out the happiness of men who are always rolling, with dark fear and cruel lust, in warlike slaughters and in blood, which, whether shed in civil or foreign war, is still human blood; so that their joy may be compared to glass in its fragile splendor, of which one is horribly afraid lest it should be suddenly broken in pieces.

That this may be more easily discerned, let us not come to nought by being carried away with empty boasting, or blunt the edge of our attention by loud-sounding names of things, when we hear of peoples, kingdoms, provinces. But let us suppose a case of two men; for each individual man, like one letter in a language, is as it were the element of a city or kingdom, however far-spreading in its occupation of the earth. Of these two men let us suppose that one is poor, or rather of middling circumstances; the other very rich. But the rich man is anxious with fears, pining with discontent, burning with covetousness, never secure, always uneasy, panting from the perpetual strife of his enemies, adding to his patrimony indeed by these very miseries to an immense degree, and by these additions also heaping up most bitter cares. But that other man of moderate wealth is contented with a small and compact estate, most dear to his own family, enjoying the sweetest peace with his kindred neighbors and friends, in piety religious, benignant in mind, healthy in body, in life frugal, in manners chaste, in conscience secure.

I know not whether any one can be such a fool, that he dare hesitate which to prefer. As, therefore, in the case of these two men, so in two families, in two nations, in two kingdoms, this test of tranquility holds good; and if we apply it vigilantly and without prejudice, we shall quite easily see where the mere show of happiness dwells, and where real felicity. . . .

Chapter 4. Justice being taken away, then, what are kingdoms but great robberies? For what are robberies themselves, but little kingdoms? The band itself is made up of men; it is ruled by the authority of a prince, it is knit together by the pact of the confederacy; the booty is divided by the law agreed on. If, by the admittance of abandoned men, this evil increases to such a degree that it holds places, fixes abodes, takes possession of cities, and subdues peoples, it assumes the more plainly the name of a kingdom, because the reality is now manifestly conferred on it, not by the removal of covetousness, but by the addition of impunity.

Indeed, that was an apt and true reply which was given to Alexander the Great by a pirate who had been seized. For when that king had asked the man what he meant by keeping hostile possession of the sea, he answered with bold pride, "What thou meanest by seizing the whole earth; but because I do it with a petty ship, I am called a robber, whilst thou who dost it with a great fleet art styled emperor." . . .

Book 14

Chapter 28. Accordingly, two cities have been formed by two loves: the earthly by the love of the self, even to the contempt of God; the heavenly by the love of God, even to the contempt of self. The former, in a word, glories in itself, the latter in the Lord. For the one seeks glory from men; but the greatest glory of the other is God, the witness of conscience. The one lifts up its head in its own glory; the other says to its God, "Thou art my glory, and the lifter up of mine head." In the one, the princes and the nations it subdues are ruled by the love of ruling; in the other, the princes and the subjects serve one another in love, the latter obeying, while the former take thought for all. The one delights in its own strength, represented in the persons of its rulers; the other says to its God, "I will love Thee, O Lord, my strength." And therefore the wise men of the one city, living according to man, have sought for profit to their own bodies or souls, or both, and those who have known God "glorified Him not as God, neither were thankful, but became vain in their imaginations, and their foolish heart was darkened; professing themselves to be wise,"—that is, glorying in their wisdom, and being possessed by pride,—"they became fools, and changed the glory of the incorruptible God into an image made like to corruptible man, and to birds, and four-footed beasts, and creeping things." For they were either leaders or followers of the people in adoring images, "and worshipped and served the creature more than the Creator, who is blessed for ever." But in the other city there is not human wisdom, but only godliness, which offers due worship to the true God, and looks for its reward in the society of the saints, of holy angels as well as holy men, "that God may be all in all."

Book 15

Chapter 1. . . . Of [the] two first parents of the human race . . . Cain was the first-born, and he belonged to the city of men; after him was born Abel, who belonged to the city of God. For as in the individual the truth of the apostle's statement is discerned, "that is not first which is spiritual, but that which is natural, and afterward that which is spiritual," whence it comes to pass that each man, being derived from a condemned stock, is first of all born of Adam evil and carnal, and becomes good and spiritual only afterwards, when he is grafted into Christ by regeneration: so was it in the human race as a whole. When these two cities began to run their course by a series of deaths and births, the citizen of this world was the first-born, and after him the stranger in this world, the citizen of the city of God, predestinated by grace, elected by grace, by grace a stranger below, and by grace a citizen above. By grace,—for so far as regards himself he is sprung from the same mass, all of which is condemned in its origin: but God, like a potter (for this comparison is introduced by the apostle judiciously, and not without thought), of the same lump made one vessel to honor, another to dishonor. But first the vessel to dishonor was made, and after it another to honor. For in each individual, as I have already said, there is first of all that which is reprobate, that from which we must begin, but in which we need not necessarily remain; afterwards is that which is well-approved, to which we may by advancing attain, and in which, when we have reached it, we may abide. Not, indeed, that every wicked man shall be good, but that no one will be good who was not first of all wicked;

but the sooner any one becomes a good man, the more speedily does he receive this title, and abolish the old name in the new.

Accordingly, it is recorded of Cain that he built a city, but Abel, being a sojourner, built none. For the city of the saints is above, although here below it begets citizens, in whom it sojourns till the time of its reign arrives, when it shall gather together all in the day of the resurrection; and then shall the promised kingdom be given to them, in which they shall reign with their Prince, the King of the ages, time without end.

Translated by Marcus Dods. From *Nicene and Post-Nicene Fathers,* 1st Series, edited by Philip Schaff (New York: Christian Literature Company, 1886–1890), Volume 11, pages 65–66, 282–285.

CHAPTER 6

The Early Middle Ages

Augustine died as a barbarian army surrounded his city, a symbol of the tough future western Europe—and its theology—faced. Most of Europe soon lost the easy trade, communication, and advanced urban life that had survived even in the late Roman Empire. Much of the period from about 400 to 1000 was indeed a "Dark Age." After the collapse of the Roman Empire, the church was often the strongest institution around, and it naturally undertook some of the work of governing. On the other hand, in the medieval world income came from land, and landowners had to swear fealty to a lord who gave them protection. So a local bishop was often the vassal of a secular overlord. Keeping political and religious authority straight proved complicated.

In earlier centuries, Christian theologians had worked to relate their faith to an intellectually sophisticated culture; now they faced the task of presenting the faith in simple, vivid terms to often uneducated people. To do this, they told stories of heroic martyrs and saints and especially encouraged the veneration of the Virgin Mary; they developed a system of penance to regulate moral life; and they emphasized Christ's presence in the sacraments.

All that made faith more concrete, but it also raised new theological questions to importance. Could Christians, should Christians, pray to saints and honor their relics? How did the insistence on Christian moral standards and the discipline of penance fit with Augustine's claim that salvation comes by unmerited grace? How exactly was Christ present in the bread and wine of the Eucharist? In the centuries from Augustine's death until about 1100 no theologian came close to Augustine in stature, but on matters as diverse as saints, sacraments, Mary, grace, and the power of church and state, theologians during this period sorted out a great many practical questions in a way that would continue to influence the life of the church.

Pope Gelasius I (d. 496)

From *Letter to the Emperor Anastasius*

Gelasius was Pope from 492 to 496. In 482 the Emperor Zeno had attempted to resolve a dispute between orthodox Christians and Monophysites by drawing up a compromise statement—a precursor of the Typos *discussed in Chapter 4. Addressing Zeno's successor Anastasius, Gelasius seeks to make clear that such doctrinal matters are none of the emperor's business. The relation of church and state in the Middle Ages is an immensely complicated question and cannot be properly presented in a collection of documents from the history of theology, but this text did lay the theological foundation for many of the debates that would follow.*

There are two powers, august Emperor, by which this world is ruled from the beginning: the consecrated authority of the bishops and the royal power. In these matters the priests bear the heavier burden because they will render account, even for rulers of men, at the divine judgment. Besides, most gracious son, you are aware that, although you in your office are the ruler of the human race, nevertheless you devoutly bow your head before those who are leaders in things divine and look to them for the means of your salvation; and in the reception and proper administration of the heavenly sacraments you know that you ought to submit to Christian order rather than take the lead, and in those matters follow their judgment without wanting to subject them to your will. For if, in matters relating to public law and order, Christian priests themselves obey your laws in the knowledge that your Empire is conferred upon you by heavenly disposition, and lest they appear to be resisting your judgment, which is unchallengeable in worldly affairs, then how eagerly one ought to obey those who are assigned to the administration of the hallowed mysteries! There is no slight danger to the bishops in not having spoken up for the worship of God as they should; and, which God forbid, there is no inconsiderable peril in store for those who behave contemptuously when they ought to be obedient. And if it be right that the hearts of the faithful should submit to all bishops everywhere who rightly administer the things that are divine, how much more then must they give their support to the bishop of this see, who, even by the supreme divine will, was to be superior to all other priests, and whom the Church has obediently honored with universal loyalty.

Pope Gelasius I

From *Tractatus IV*

Before the coming of Christ it happened that certain men, although at that time they were only appointed to carry out worldly functions, were in a sense both kings and priests, because Scripture tells us that the holy Melchisedech was such a person [Gen. 14:17–20]. And the devil imitated this among his own people, since he always strives to claim for himself, like a usurper, things pertaining to the worship of God, with the result that heathen Emperors were also called Supreme Pontiffs. But after the coming of the true King and Pontiff, the Emperor no longer assumed the title of Pontiff, nor did the Pontiff lay claim to the royal supremacy. For even though the body of the true King and Pontiff is said to have embraced both these attributes in holy nobility, according to their participation in his majestic nature, so that a nation may be at once royal and priestly, yet Christ, thinking of human frailty, by a majestic disposition took the appropriate measure for the salvation of his people, and distinguished the sphere of each power by appropriate functions and distinct titles, wishing his people to be saved by the physic of humility and not be struck down again by human arrogance. Hence at the same time Christian Emperors needed bishops for the sake of eternal life, and bishops availed themselves of imperial decrees for the good order of temporal affairs. Hence the spiritual function might be immune from worldly interference, and "No soldier of God might involve himself in the affairs of this life" [2 Tim. 2:4], and conversely no man who was involved in the affairs of this life might take charge of things divine. Hence both orders might be restrained and neither be boosted and exalted above the other, and each calling might become specially competent in certain kinds of function.

Jerome (345–420)

From *Against Vigilantius*

Trained in the tradition of classical rhetoric, Jerome turned to a life of Christian asceticism. He is best known as the translator of the Vulgate, the standard Latin version of the Bible, but those who read his works may remember him most for the violence of his polemics. Christians had begun to pray to the saints and honor their relics. Vigilantius, who was from Gaul and was born about 370, had written a treatise criticizing the emerging cult of the saints for introducing elements of pagan superstition into Christian faith. Jerome's reply in this treatise was written in the course of a single night in 406. He began by noting the irony that Vigilantius, whose name means "wakeful," should oppose vigils in honor of the saints—his name might better be "sleepyhead."

1. . . . All at once Vigilantius, or, more correctly, *Dormitantius,* has arisen, animated by an unclean spirit, to fight against the Spirit of Christ, and to deny that religious reverence is to be paid to the tombs of the martyrs. Vigils, he says, are to be condemned. . . .

4. . . . Among other blasphemies, he may be heard to say, "What need is there for you not only to pay such honor, not to say adoration, to the thing, whatever it may be, which you carry about in a little vessel and worship?" . . . And again, in the same book, "Under the cloak of religion we see what is all but a heathen ceremony introduced into the churches: while the sun is still shining, heaps of tapers are lighted, and everywhere a paltry bit of powder, wrapped up in a costly cloth, is kissed and worshipped. Great honor do men of this sort pay to the blessed martyrs, who, they think, are to be made glorious by trumpery tapers, when the Lamb who is in the midst of the throne, with all the brightness of His majesty, gives them light."

5. . . . Tell us more clearly (that there may be no restraint on your blasphemy) what you mean by the phrase "a bit of powder wrapped up in a costly cloth in a tiny vessel." It is nothing less than the relics of the martyrs which he is vexed to see covered with a costly veil, and not bound up with rags or hair-cloth, or thrown on the midden, so that Vigilantius alone in his drunken stupor may be worshipped. Are we, therefore, guilty of sacrilege when we enter the basilica of

the Apostles?* Was the Emperor Constantius I guilty of sacrilege when he transferred the sacred relics of Andrew, Luke, and Timothy to Constantinople? . . .

6. For you say that the souls of the Apostles and martyrs have their abode either in the bosom of Abraham, or in the place of refreshment, or under the altar of God, and that they cannot leave their own tombs, and be present where they will. . . . Will you lay down the law for God? Will you put the Apostles into chains? So that to the day of judgement they are to be kept in confinement, and are not with their Lord, although it is written concerning them, "They follow the Lamb, whithersoever he goeth" [Rev. 14:4]. If the Lamb is present everywhere, the same must be believed respecting those who are with the Lamb. And while the devil and the demons wander through the whole world, and with only too great speed present themselves everywhere; are martyrs, after the shedding of their blood, to be kept out of sight shut up in a coffin, from whence they cannot escape? You say, in your pamphlet, that so long as we are alive we can pray for one another; but once we die the prayer of no person for another can be heard, and all the more because the martyrs, though they cry for the avenging of their blood, have never been able to obtain their request. If Apostles and martyrs while still in the body can pray for others, when they ought still to be anxious for themselves, how much more must they do so when once they have won their crowns, overcome, and triumphed?

Translated by W. H. Freemantle. From *Nicene and Post-Nicene Fathers,* 2nd Series, edited by Philip Schaff and Henry Wace (New York: Christian Literature Company, 1890–1900), Volume 6, pages 417–419.

Jerome

From *The Perpetual Virginity of Blessed Mary*

None of the saints received quite the veneration accorded the Virgin Mary, whose cult both reflected and encouraged the honor increasingly paid to celibacy and virginity. A certain Helvidius had written a treatise arguing that Mary had had other children after the birth of Jesus, citing as his principal evidence the Gospel references to Jesus' brothers and sisters. Jerome's reply, written about 383, addressed not

---

*Where relics were given a place of honor.

only questions about Mary but also attitudes toward marriage and sexuality.

1. I was requested by certain of the brethren not long ago to reply to a pamphlet written by one Helvidius. I have deferred doing so, not because it is a difficult matter to maintain the truth and refute an ignorant boor who has scarce known the first glimmer of learning, but because I was afraid my reply might make him appear worth defeating. . . .

2. I must call upon the Holy Spirit to express His meaning by my mouth and defend the virginity of the Blessed Mary. I must call upon the Lord Jesus to guard the sacred lodging of the womb in which He abode for ten months from all suspicion of sexual intercourse. And I must also entreat God the Father to show that the mother of His Son, who was a mother before she was a bride, continued a Virgin after her son was born. . . .

Jerome recalls the biblical report that Joseph did not seek intercourse with Mary before the birth of Jesus because he had been warned in a dream.

8. . . . We are to believe then that the same man who gave so much credit to a dream that he did not dare to touch his wife, yet afterwards, when he had learnt from the shepherds that the angel of the Lord had come from heaven and said to them, "Be not afraid; for behold I bring you good tidings of great joy which shall be to all people, for there is born to you this day in the city of David a Savior, which is Christ the Lord"; . . . and when he had seen Anna the prophetess, the Magi, the Star, Herod, the angels; Helvidius, I say, would have us believe that Joseph, though well acquainted with such surprising wonders, dared to touch the temple of God, the abode of the Holy Ghost, the mother of his Lord? . . .

13. The last proposition of Helvidius was . . . that brethren of the Lord are mentioned in the Gospels. . . .

16. . . . How, then, says, Helvidius, do you make out that they were called the Lord's brethren who were not his brethren? I will show how that is. In Holy Scripture there are four kinds of brethren—by nature, race, kindred, love. . . .

17. . . . I now ask to which class you consider the Lord's brethren in the Gospel must be assigned. They are brethren by nature, you say. But Scripture does not say so; it calls them neither sons of Mary, nor

of Joseph. Shall we say they are brethren by race? But it is absurd to suppose that a few Jews were called His brethren when all Jews of the time might upon this principle have borne the title. Were they brethren by virtue of close intimacy and the union of heart and mind? If that were so, who were more truly His brethren than the apostles who received his private instruction? . . . The only alternative is to adopt the previous explanation and understand them to be called brethren in virtue of the bond of kindred . . . just as Abraham himself had to wife Sarah his sister, for he says, "She is indeed my sister on the father's side, not on the mother's" [Gen. 20:11], that is to say, she was the daughter of his brother. . . .

22. And now that I am about to institute a comparison between virginity and marriage, I beseech my readers not to suppose that in praising virginity I have in the least disparaged marriage, and separated the saints of the Old Testament from those of the New, that is to say, those who had wives and those who altogether refrained from the embraces of women: I rather think that in accordance with the difference in time and circumstance one rule applied to the former, another to us upon whom the ends of the world have come. So long as that law remained, "Be fruitful and multiply and replenish the earth" [Gen. 1:28], and "Cursed is the barren woman that beareth not seed in Israel" [probably a mistranslation of Ex. 23:26], they all married and were given in marriage, left father and mother, and became one flesh. But once in tones of thunder the words were heard, "The time is shortened, that henceforth those that have wives may be as though they had none" [1 Cor. 7:29]: cleaving to the Lord, we are made one spirit with Him. And why? Because "He that is unmarried is careful for the things of the Lord, how he may please the Lord: but he that is married is careful for the things of the world, how he may please his wife. And there is a difference also between the wife and the virgin. She that is unmarried is careful for the things of the Lord, that she may be holy both in body and in spirit: but she that is married is careful for the things of the world, how she may please her husband." . . . Is the sofa smooth? Is the pavement swept? Are the flowers in the cups? Is dinner ready? Tell me, pray, where amid all this is there room for the thought of God? . . .

23. I do not deny that holy women are found both among widows and those who have husbands; but they are such as have ceased to be wives, or such as, even in the close bond of marriage, imitate virgin chastity.

Translated by W. H. Freemantle. From *Nicene and Post-Nicene Fathers,* 2nd Series, edited by Philip Schaff and Henry Wace (New York: Christian Literature Company, 1890–1900), Volume 6, pages 335, 338, 340–345.

Athanasius (c.298–373)

From *The Life of Antony*

This selection obviously comes out of historical sequence; though some scholars dispute his authorship, Athanasius probably wrote it around 360, in the midst of continuing debates over Arianism. But Antony became a crucial model, and this a crucial text, for the monastic and ascetic life; in that sense The Life of Antony *is one of those works that point toward the future. Antony himself was born in the middle of the third century and apparently lived, in spite of his austerities, past the age of a hundred. Athanasius evidently met him when Antony was a very old man.*

1. Antony you must know was by descent an Egyptian: his parents were of good family and possessed considerable wealth, and as they were Christians he also was reared in the same Faith. In infancy he was brought up with his parents, knowing nought else but them and his home. But when he was grown and arrived at boyhood, and was advancing in years, he could not endure to learn letters, not caring to associate with other boys; but all his desire was, as it is written of Jacob, to live a plain man at home. . . .

2. After the death of his father and mother he was left alone with one little sister: his age was about eighteen or twenty, and on him the care both of home and sister rested. Now it was not six months after the death of his parents, and going according to custom into the Lord's House, he communed with himself and reflected as he walked how the Apostles left all and followed the Savior; and how they in the Acts sold their possessions and brought and laid them at the Apostles' feet for distribution to the needy, and what and how great a hope was laid up for them in heaven. Pondering over these things he entered the church, and it happened the Gospel was being read, and he heard the Lord saying to the rich man, "If thou wouldest be perfect, go and sell that thou hast and give to the poor, and come follow Me and thou shalt have treasure in heaven" [Matt. 19:21]. Antony, as though God had put him in mind of the Saints, and the

passage had been read on his account, went out immediately from the church, and gave the possessions of his forefathers to the villages—they were three hundred acres, productive and very fair—that they should be no more a clog upon himself and his sister. And all the rest that was movable he sold, and having got together much money he gave it to the poor, reserving a little however for his sister's sake.

3. And again as he went into the church, hearing the Lord say in the Gospel, "Be not anxious for the morrow" [Matt. 6:34], he could stay no longer, but went out and gave those things also to the poor. Having committed his sister to known and faithful virgins, and put her into a convent to be brought up, he henceforth devoted himself outside his house to discipline, taking heed to himself and training himself with patience. For there were not yet so many monasteries in Egypt, and no monk at all knew of the distant desert; but all who wished to give heed to themselves practiced the discipline in solitude near their own village. . . .

5. But the devil, who hates and envies what is good, could not endure to see such a resolution in a youth, but endeavored to carry out against him what he had been wont to effect against others. . . .

7. . . . But Antony having learned from the Scriptures that the devices of the devil are many, zealously continued the discipline. . . . Wherefore more and more he repressed the body and kept it in subjection, lest haply having conquered on one side, he should be dragged down on the other. He therefore planned to accustom himself to a severer mode of life. And many marvelled, but he himself used to bear the labor easily; for the eagerness of soul, though the length of time it had abode in him, had wrought a good habit in him, so that taking but little initiation from others he showed great zeal in this matter. He kept vigil to such an extent that he often continued the whole night without sleep; and this not once but often, to the marvel of others. He ate once a day, after sunset, sometimes once in two days, and often even in four. His food was bread and salt, his drink, water only. Of flesh and wine it is superfluous even to speak, since no such thing was found with the other earnest men. A rush mat served him to sleep upon, but for the most part he lay upon the bare ground. He would not anoint himself with oil, saying it behooved young men to be earnest in training and not to seek what would enervate the body; but they must accustom it to labor, mindful

of the Apostle's words, "when I am weak, then I am strong" [2 Cor. 12:10]. . . .

93. . . . Even if this account is small compared with his merit, still from this reflect how great Antony, the man of God, was. Who from his youth to so great an age preserved a uniform zeal for the discipline, and neither through old age was subdued by the desire of costly food, nor through the infirmity of his body changed the fashion of his clothing, nor washed even his feet with water, and yet remained entirely free from harm. For his eyes were undimmed and quite sound and he saw clearly; for his teeth he had not lost one, but they had become worn to the gums through the great age of the old man. He remained strong both in hands and feet; and while all men were using various foods, and washings and diverse garments, he appeared more cheerful and of greater strength. And the fact that his fame has been blazoned everywhere; that all regard him with wonder, and that those who have never seen him long for him, is clear proof of his virtue and God's love of his soul. For not from writings, nor from worldly wisdom, nor through any art, was Antony renowned, but solely from his piety towards God.

Translated by Archibald Robertson. From *Nicene and Post-Nicene Fathers,* 2nd Series, edited by Philip Schaff and Henry Wace (New York: Christian Literature Company, 1890–1900), Volume 2, pages 195–198, 221.

Finnian of Clonard (d. c.550)

From *The Penitential of Finnian*

In the earliest church Christians confessed their sins to the whole community. It was in monastic communities, especially among the early Irish monks, that private confession to a priest and the assignment of penance became systematic. Early "penitentials" like this one tried to bring some order to the penances assigned. We know little about Finnian except that he founded a monastery and apparently died about 550.

In the name of the Father and of the Son and of the Holy Ghost.

1. If anyone has sinned in the thoughts of his heart and immediately repents, he shall beat his breast and seek pardon from God and make satisfaction, that he may be whole.

2. But if he has frequently entertained [evil] thoughts and hesitated to act on them, whether he has mastered them or been mastered by them, he shall seek pardon from God by prayer and fasting day and night until the evil thought departs and he is whole.

3. If anyone has thought evil and intended to do it, but opportunity has failed him, it is the same sin but not the same penalty; for example, if he intended fornication or murder, since the deed did not complete the intention, he has, to be sure, sinned in his heart, but if he quickly does penance, he can be helped. This penance of his is half a year on an allowance,* and he shall abstain from wine and meats for a whole year.

4. If anyone has sinned in word by an inadvertence and immediately repented, and has not said any such thing of set purpose, he ought to submit to penance, but he shall keep a special fast; moreover, thereafter let him be on his guard throughout his life, lest he commit further sin. . . .

10. But if one who is a cleric falls miserably through fornication he shall lose his place of honor, and if it happens once [only] and it is concealed from men but known before God, he shall do penance for an entire year with an allowance of bread and water and for two years abstain from wine and meats, but he shall not lose his clerical office. For, we say, sins are to be absolved in secret by penance and by very diligent devotion of heart and body.

11. If, however, he has long been in the habit of sin and it has not come to the notice of men, he shall do penance for three years with bread and water and lose his clerical office, and for three years more he shall abstain from wine and meats, since it is not a smaller thing to sin before God than before men. . . .

14. But if one of the clerical order is on familiar terms with any woman and he has himself done no evil with her, neither by cohabiting with her nor by lascivious embraces, this is his penance: For such time as he has done this he shall withdraw from the communion of the altar and do penance for forty days and nights with bread and water and cast out of his heart his fellowship with the woman, and so be restored to the altar.

From *Medieval Handbooks of Penance,* translated by John T. McNeill and Helen M. Gamer (New York: Octagon Books, 1965), pages 87–89. Copyright © 1938 by Columbia University Press. Used by permission of Columbia University Press.

---

*A specified, and limited, amount of food.

John Cassian (360–435)

From *The Third Conference of Abbot Chaeremon*

Cassian began his monastic career in Egypt but moved to France and helped make the monastic life influential in the West. While Augustine deeply influenced medieval theology, many grew nervous about his radical claims concerning predestination. Historians classify Cassian as a "semi-Pelagian." He believed grace essential to salvation and thought that God simply seizes some and saves them, but he also thought that ordinarily God rewards human efforts and that God wants to save everyone and is prevented only by those who reject grace.

Chapter 6. . . . In everything, it can be shown that men always have need of God's help, and that human weakness cannot accomplish anything that has to do with salvation by itself alone, i.e., without the aid of God. . . . Who, I ask, could, however fervent he might be in spirit, relying on his own strength with no praise from men endure the squalor of the desert, and I will not say the daily lack but the supply of dry bread? Who without the Lord's consolation, could put up with the continual thirst for water, or deprive his human eyes of that sweet and delicious morning sleep, and regularly compress his whole time of rest and repose into the limits of four hours? Who would be sufficient without God's grace to give continual attendance to reading and constant earnestness in work, receiving no advantage of present gain? And all these matters, as we cannot desire them continuously without divine inspiration, so in no respect whatever can we perform them without His help. . . .

Chapter 7. For the purpose of God whereby He made man not to perish but to live for ever, stands immovable. And when His goodness sees in us even the very smallest spark of good will shining forth, which He Himself has struck as it were out of the hard flints of our hearts, He fans and fosters it and nurses it with His breath, as He "willeth all men to be saved and to come to the knowledge of the truth," for as He says, "it is not the will of your Father which is in heaven that one of these little ones should perish," and again it says, "Neither will God have a soul to perish, but recalleth," meaning that he that is cast off should not altogether perish [1 Tim. 2:4; Matt. 18:14; 2 Sam. 14:14]. For He is true, and lieth not when He lays down with an oath: "as I live, saith the Lord God, for I will not the death of a sinner, but that he should turn from his way and live" [Ezek. 33:11]. For if He willeth not that one of His little ones should perish, how can we imagine without grievous blasphemy that He does not generally will *all* men, but only *some* instead of *all* to be saved? Those then who perish, perish against His will. . . . "They have hardened their faces and refused to return" [Jer. 8:5]. The grace of Christ then is at hand every day, which, while it "willeth all men to be saved and to come to the knowledge of the truth," calleth all without any exception, saying: "Come unto Me, all ye that labor and are heavy laden, and I will refresh you" [Matt. 11:28]. But if He calls not all generally but only some, it follows that not all are heavy laden either with original or actual sin, and that this saying is not a true one: "For all have sinned and come short of the glory of God"; nor can we believe that "death passed on all men" [Rom. 3:23; 5:12]. And so far do all who perish, perish against the will of God, that God cannot be said to have made death, and Scripture itself testifies: "For God made not death, neither rejoiceth in the destruction of the living" [Wisd. of Sol. 1:13]. . . .

Chapter 11. . . . Does God have compassion upon us because we have shown the beginning of a good will, or does the beginning of a good will follow because God has had compassion upon us? For many believing each of these and asserting them more widely than is right are entangled in all kinds of opposite errors. For if we say that the beginning of free will is in our own power, what about Paul the persecutor, what about Matthew the publican, of whom the one was drawn to salvation while eager for bloodshed and the punishment of the innocent, the other for violence and rapine? But if we say that the beginning of our free will is always due to the inspiration of the grace of God, what about the faith of Zaccheus, or what are we to say of the goodness of the thief on the cross, who by their own desires brought violence to bear on the kingdom of heaven and so prevented the special leadings of their vocation? But if we attribute the performance of virtuous acts, and the execution of God's commands to our own will, how do we pray: "Strengthen, O God, what Thou hast wrought in us"; and "The work of our hands stablish Thou upon us"? [Ps. 68:29; 90:17]. . . .

These two then; viz., the grace of God and free will seem opposed to each other, but really are in harmony, and we gather from the system of goodness that we ought to have both alike, lest if we withdraw one of them from man, we may seem to have broken the rule of the Church's faith: for when God sees us inclined to will what is good, He meets, guides, and strengthens us: for "At the voice of thy cry, as soon as He shall hear, He will answer thee"; and: "Call upon Me," He says, "in the way of tribulation and I will deliver thee, and thou shalt glorify Me" [Isa. 30:19; Ps. 50:15]. And again, if He finds that we are unwilling or have grown cold, He stirs our hearts with salutary exhortations, by which a good will is either renewed or formed in us. . . .

Chapter 13. And so the grace of God always co-operates with our will for its advantage, and in all things assists, protects, and defends it, in such a way as sometimes even to require and look for some efforts of good will from it that it may not appear to confer its gifts on one who is asleep or relaxed in sluggish ease, as it seeks opportunities to show that as the torpor of man's sluggishness is shaken off its bounty is not unreasonable, when it bestows it on account of some desire and efforts to gain it. And none the less does God's grace continue to be free grace while in return for some small and trivial efforts it bestows with priceless bounty such glory of immortality, and such gifts of eternal bliss.

Translated by Edgar C. S. Gibson. From *Nicene and Post-Nicene Fathers,* 2nd Series, edited by Philip Schaff and Henry Wace (New York: Christian Literature Company, 1890–1900), Volume 11, pages 424–425, 427–428, 430.

Florus of Lyons (?) (c.790–c.860)

From *Reply to the Three Letters*

In the ninth century a Saxon monk named Gottschalk (c.805–868) grew convinced that Augustine was right about unmerited grace and predestination and that by Augustinian standards the ninth-century church had fallen into Pelagianism. Thrown into prison, he refused to recant his views. Hincmar of Reims and Rabanus Maurus of Mainz, among others, wrote letters attacking Gottschalk. This treatise, which sets out to defend him, was written about 850, traditionally by Remigius, the bishop of Lyons. But recent scholarship suggests that the real author may have been Florus, a deacon in the church at Lyons.

2. . . . In God there is no new will, no new plan, no new arrangement, no new decision, as though from eternity he was not with

himself and in himself but only afterward came into existence. Nothing is accidental to his divinity and in his deity nothing can be increased, diminished, or changed. Therefore whatever he foreknew, he foreknew from all eternity; whatever he foreordained, he doubtless foreordained from all eternity. . . . In this way too the psalmist, showing forth the appropriate portion of the elect and of the reprobate, that is, by the eternal decree of God the former predestined to mercy, the latter to perdition, speaks clearly and openly of the elect, "The mercy of the Lord is from everlasting to everlasting upon those who fear him" [Ps. 103:17], but of the reprobate, "Those who withdraw themselves far from you shall perish in their wickedness; you have destroyed all those who have gone awhoring from you" [Ps. 73:27]. . . .

10. With one meaning, one mouth, one spirit, the most blessed fathers of the church proclaim and commend the immovable truth of divine foreknowledge and foreordination in both instances, namely, of the elect and of the reprobate; of the elect to glory, of the reprobate not to guilt but to punishment. Herein they boldly state that there is demonstrated for us an immutable order, not of temporal arrangements, nor of those beginning at a particular time, but of the everlasting designs of God. They affirm, moreover, that none of the elect can perish and that, because of the hardness and impenitence of their hearts, none of the reprobate can be saved. . . . For according to the catholic faith Almighty God, even before the establishment of the world, before he made anything, did from the beginning by his own free benevolence predestine certain ones to the kingdom by the sure, just, and unchangeable motives of his own eternal counsel. Of these none will perish since his mercy defends them. He predestined others by his own just judgment to death because of the desert of their impiety which he foresaw. Of these none can be saved, not because of any ferocity of divine power, but because of the untameable and constant villainy of their own wickedness. . . .

47. . . . First, no one says that his creator, the highest God, is malevolent (heaven forbid!) as though He were ill-willed toward his creation, for his will is ever good to the good. If it seems evil to the evil, it is nonetheless always just and therefore cannot be evil. . . .

Secondly, no one who faithfully believes and acknowledges divine predestination to each lot, that is, of the elect and of the reprobate, endeavors to prove that Truth himself is deceptive, but rather is absolutely true and trustworthy in all his words and holy in all his works, because to the elect, as he has foreordained, he promises and assigns the rewards of everlasting life. On the other hand, to sinful and impenitent reprobates he repays everlasting punishments by his own just decree as he has foreordained.

Thirdly, the truth of divine predestination does not proclaim the just judge to be unjust, since according to it rewards are returned to those who do good and continue in good, and torments are inflicted upon those who do evil and remain in evil.

Fourthly, no necessity of his own predestination renders the Redeemer of the world unable through the glorious worth of his own blood to come to the aid of those who believe and hope in him, for by that price he forever comes to the aid of all his elect. Because he does not come to the aid of the reprobate, they through their own evil and unrighteousness spurn his price. Even if he can save them, he nevertheless wishes by a just vengeance to condemn some for the purpose of showing forth the terror of his sternness.

From *Early Medieval Theology,* edited and translated by George E. McCracken (Volume IX: The Library of Christian Classics), pages 157–159, 173–174. First published in MCMLVII by the SCM Press Ltd., London, and The Westminster Press, Philadelphia. Used by permission of the publishers.

John Scotus Eriugena (c.810–c.866)

From *On the Division of Nature*

In the early Middle Ages learning survived in Ireland more than anywhere else in the West. Eriugena knew Greek and read widely in the history of theology; his theology shows influences that go back to Pseudo-Dionysius the Areopagite and Origen. As this selection indicates, even in the ninth century speculative theology on a grand scale did not entirely disappear.

[God] is the principle of all things that were created by him and he is also the end of all things that were created by him and he is also the end of all things that seek him in order that they may find their rest. Indeed, the cause of all can be said to create when those things created by him and after him, by a kind of marvelous divine multiplication proceed to become genera, species, and individuals and all the other various things which are considered as established in nature. But because all those things which came forth from this selfsame cause will return to it as their end, it is designated as the goal of all and is referred to as neither creating nor created. For once all things will have returned to it, nothing further will come forth from it to become genera and forms generated in time and space; in it all will remain at rest, and one, immutable individual. . . .

If the Word of the Father, in whom all things are and in whom all things have been made, is the cause of all things visible and invisible, is he not also the "cause of causes" or finis of the world, in whom it will come to an end? Is there any goal beyond him that any creature could desire? . . .

That is why we can sum up what we have tried by many arguments to suggest, defining him thus: the one from whom and unto whom are all things, for he is both beginning and end. This too is what the Apostle most obviously infers when he says: "For from him and through him and unto him are all things" [Rom. 11:36]. Here we have most clearly propounded on apostolic authority, as Maximus points out in his *Ambiguities* [Chapter 37], not only the origin of all that was made, by the fivefold divisions, but also the return and reunion through the selfsame divisions and the resolution of the whole of creation into one and ultimately into God himself. . . .

In the resurrection sexual differences will disappear and nature will be reunited so that there will just be man as he would have been had he not sinned. Next, the earth will be rejoined to paradise and there will be only paradise. Then the earth will be reunited to the heavens and there will be only the heavens. . . . Then the whole of sensible creation's reunion and transmutation into what is intelligible takes place, so that every creature will become intelligible. Afterwards the whole creation will be united with the Creator and it will be one in him and with him. And this represents the destiny or goal of all things visible and invisible, because all things visible are transformed into intelligibles and the intelligibles into God by a marvelous and ineffable union, but not—as we have frequently insisted—by a confusion or annihilation of their essences or substances. Then God will be all in all, when there is nothing but God. Not that we are trying to say that the substance of things will perish, but that they will return through the aforementioned stages to become something better. And how can anything perish when it turns into something better? Hence the change of human nature into God should not be thought of as a destruction of its substance, but as a wonderful and ineffable return to that pristine state it lost through sin.

Paschasius Radbertus (c.785–c.860)

From *The Lord's Body and Blood*

Radbertus served for a time as abbot of the French monastery of Corbie. He insisted in this treatise that in the Eucharist the bread and wine become the true body and blood of Christ. Two hundred years later, with the introduction of Aristotelian terminology, theologians began to describe the process as "transubstantiation"—the elements retain the "accidents" of bread and wine, such as taste and texture, but take on the substance of Christ's body and blood. Radbertus lacked that technical terminology but wanted to insist in the strongest way on a real transformation.

Chapter 1. 2. It is . . . clear that nothing is possible outside the will of God or contrary to it, but all things wholly yield to him. Therefore, let no man be moved from this body and blood of Christ which in a mystery are true flesh and true blood since the Creator so willed it. . . . As the Truth himself said to his disciples: "This is my flesh for the life of the world" [John 6:51], and, to put it in more miraculous terms, nothing different, of course, from what was born of Mary, suffered on the cross, and rose again from the tomb. . . .

If our words seem unbelievable to anyone, let him note all the miracles of the Old and New Testament which, through firm faith, were accomplished by God contrary to natural order, and he will see clearer than day that for God nothing is impossible, since all things that God wills to be, and whatsoever he wills, actually take place. . . .

Chapter 3. 1. A sacrament is anything handed down to us in any divine celebration as a pledge of salvation, when what is visibly done accomplishes inwardly something far different, to be taken in a holy sense. They are called sacraments either because they are secret in that in the visible act divinity inwardly accomplishes something secretly through the corporeal appearance, or from the sanctifying consecration, because the Holy Spirit, remaining in the body of Christ, latently accomplishes for the salvation of the faithful all these mystical sacraments under the cover of things visible. By this divine power he teaches the souls of believers about things invisible more than if he visibly revealed what inwardly is effective for salvation. "For we walk by faith and not by sight" [2 Cor. 5:7].

2. Christ's sacraments in the church are Baptism and anointing, and the Lord's body and blood, which are called sacraments because under their visible appearance the divine flesh is secretly hallowed through power, so that they are inwardly in truth what they are outwardly believed to be by the power of faith. . . .

Chapter 4. 1. That in truth the body and blood are created by the consecration of the mystery, no one doubts who believes the divine words when the Truth says: "For my flesh is truly food, and my blood is truly drink" [John 6:55]. And that when his disciples did not rightly understand, he clearly identified what flesh he meant, what blood: "He who eats my flesh and drinks my blood, abides in me and I in him" [John 6:56]. Therefore, if it is truly food, it is true flesh, and if it is truly drink, it is true blood. How else will what he says be true: "The bread which I shall give, my flesh, is for the life of the world" [John 6:51], unless it be true flesh? and the "bread which came down from heaven" [John 6:51], true bread? But because it is not right to devour Christ with the teeth, he willed in the mystery that this bread and wine be created truly his flesh and blood through consecration by the power of the Holy Spirit, by daily creating it so that it might be mystically sacrificed for the life of the world; so that as from the Virgin through the Spirit true flesh is created without union of sex, so through the same, out of the substance of bread and wine, the same body and blood of Christ may be mystically consecrated.

From *Early Medieval Theology,* edited and translated by George E. McCracken (Volume IX: The Library of Christian Classics), pages 94, 98–99, 101. First published in MCMLVII by the SCM Press Ltd., London, and The Westminster Press, Philadelphia. Used by permission of the publishers.

Ratramnus of Corbie (d. c.868)

From *Christ's Body and Blood*

Ratramnus, like Radbertus, lived in the monastery of Corbie. He disagreed with his fellow monk; Ratramnus thought that the bread and wine are only mystic symbols of Christ's body and blood. This selection, from a treatise addressed to King Charles the Bald, shows not only his Eucharistic views but also some interesting ideas on the use of religious language. Some theologians in the Reformation returned to Ratramnus' ideas, but in the short run at least he lost the argument.

5. Your majesty inquires whether that which in the church is received into the mouth of the faithful becomes the body and blood of Christ in a mystery or in truth. That is, whether it contains some hidden element which becomes patent only to the eyes of faith, or whether without concealment of any mystery the appearance of the body is seen outwardly in what the mind's eyes see inwardly, so that everything which takes place becomes clearly visible; and whether it is that body which was born of Mary, suffered, died, and was buried, and which, rising again and ascending into heaven, sits on the right hand of the Father.

6. Let us examine the first of these two questions, and, to prevent our being stopped by ambiguity of language, let us define what we mean by "figure," what by "truth," so that keeping our gaze fixed on something quite certain, we may know in what path of reasoning we ought to direct our steps.

7. "Figure" means a kind of overshadowing that reveals its intent under some sort of veil. For example, when we wish to speak of the Word, we say, "bread," as when in the Lord's Prayer we ask that daily bread be given us, or when Christ speaking in the Gospel says, "I am the living bread who came down from heaven" [John 6:41]; or when he calls himself the vine and his disciples the branches [John 15:5]. For all these passages say one thing and hint at another.

8. "Truth," on the other hand, is representation of clear fact, not obscured by any shadowy images, but uttered in pure and open, and to say it more plainly, in natural meanings, as, for example, when Christ is said to have been born of the Virgin, suffered, been crucified, died, and been buried. For nothing is here adumbrated by concealing

metaphors, but the reality of the fact is represented in the ordinary senses of the words. Nothing else may be understood than what is said. In the instances mentioned above this was not the case. From the point of view of substance, the bread is not Christ, the vine is not Christ, the branches are not apostles. Therefore in this latter instance the figure, but in the former the truth, is represented by the statement, that is, the bare and obvious meaning.

9. Now let us go back to the matter which is the cause of what has been said, namely, the body and blood of Christ. For if that mystery is not performed in any figurative sense, then it is not rightly given the name of mystery. Since that cannot be called a mystery in which there is nothing hidden, nothing removed from the physical senses, nothing covered over with any veil. But that bread which through the ministry of the priest comes to be Christ's body exhibits one thing outwardly to human sense, and it proclaims another thing inwardly to the minds of the faithful. Outwardly it has the shape of bread which it had before, the color is exhibited, the flavor is received, but inwardly something far different, much more precious, much more excellent, becomes known, because something heavenly, something divine, that is, Christ's body, is revealed, which is not beheld, or received, or consumed by the fleshly senses but in the gaze of the believing soul.

10. The wine also, which through priestly consecration becomes the sacrament of Christ's blood, shows, so far as the surface goes, one thing; inwardly it contains something else. What else is to be seen on the surface than the substance of wine? Taste it, and it has the flavor of wine; smell it, and it has the aroma of wine; look at it, and the wine color is visible. But if you think of it inwardly, it is now to the minds of believers not the liquid of Christ's blood, and when tasted, it has flavor; when looked at, it has appearance; and when smelled, it is proved to be such. Since no one can deny that this is so, it is clear that that bread and wine are Christ's body and blood in a figurative sense. For as to outward appearance, the aspect of flesh is not recognized in that bread, nor in that wine is the liquid blood shown, when, however, they are, after the mystical consecration, no longer called bread or wine, but Christ's body and blood.

11. For if, as some would have it, nothing is here received figuratively, but everything is visible in truth, faith does not operate here, since nothing spiritual takes place, but whatever it is, it is wholly received according to its bodily sense. And since faith, according to the apostle, is "the evidence of things not appearing" [Heb. 11:1],

that is, not of substances, visible but invisible, we shall here receive nothing according to faith since we distinguish what it is according to the senses of the body. Nothing is more absurd than to take bread as flesh and to say that wine is blood, and there will be no mystery in anything which contains nothing secret, nothing concealed. . . .

49. From all that has thus far been said it has been shown that Christ's body and blood which are received in the mouth of the faithful in the church are figures according to their visible appearance, but according to their invisible substance, that is, the power of the divine Word, truly exist as Christ's body and blood. Therefore, with respect to the visible creation, they feed the body; with reference to the power of a stronger substance, they feed and sanctify the souls of the faithful.

From *Early Medieval Theology,* edited and translated by George E. McCracken (Volume IX: The Library of Christian Classics), pages 119–121, 132. First published in MCMLVII by the SCM Press Ltd., London, and The Westminster Press, Philadelphia. Used by permission of the publishers.

CHAPTER 7

The High Middle Ages

In the eleventh, twelfth, and thirteenth centuries new schools and universities, wider scholarly debate, and the translation of Aristotle's scientific and philosophical texts into Latin created a richer intellectual context for the doing of theology. But they also posed new problems in relating what reason discovered to what faith believed.

At the same time practical reforms were reshaping many Christian lives. The developed system of sacraments provided Christian people with a path toward salvation, but new questions emerged about the way in which Christ's incarnation, suffering, and death achieve the salvation of others. At the beginning of the thirteenth century, Dominic and Francis established new orders of "friars" dedicated to the monastic tradition of self-denial but preaching among the people instead of withdrawing to monasteries. The Franciscan commitment to poverty raised awkward questions about the wealth of the church, and widespread corruption created pressure for reform at the same time that questions arose about the relation of church and state power.

In the late eleventh century, Anselm of Canterbury, the first truly great theologian of the period, had held the forces of reason and faith together. Following the Augustinian motto of "faith seeking understanding," he began with faith but probed its logic with reason as daringly as anyone ever has. Anselm, however, operated in the context of a monastic school; a generation later Peter Abelard worked amid the skeptical give-and-take of the University of Paris, where the application of reason seemed inevitably to lead to questions about faith.

The availability of many of Aristotle's works in Latin beginning in the twelfth century exacerbated these tensions. Theologians had been teaching that the way to truth begins by turning inward, but Aristotle pursued knowledge by beginning with sense experience. Theologians had taught that understanding should begin with Christian faith, but Aristotle seemed to have understood a great deal without being a Christian. Thomas Aquinas faced these and other problems. He constructed arguments for the existence of God that began with sense experience. Truths known to reason, he said, are distinct from truths known only to faith. Both come ultimately from God, but the two realms have independent integrity.

In a society debating the relation of church and state, that claim had potentially radical implications, for, if reason has an authority independent of faith, should not the state have an authority independent of the church? On this issue, as on many others, theology in this period, which often seems to us a time of intellectual stability and consensus, underwent deep turmoil.

Anselm of Canterbury (1033–1109)

From *Proslogion*

Anselm was born in northern Italy, studied and lived in a French monastery, and ended his life as Archbishop of Canterbury in England. As the first section quoted here indicates, he stood in the Augustinian tradition, which held that understanding should begin with faith. He here offers the most famous version of the "ontological argument for the existence of God," an argument based purely on the logic of God's way of being ("onto-" comes from a form of the Greek verb "to be"). Several contemporary philosophers have noted that this passage really presents two arguments—in Chapter 2 for God's existence, and in Chapter 3 for God's necessary existence.

Chapter 1. . . . I am not trying, O Lord, to penetrate thy loftiness, for I cannot begin to match my understanding with it, but I desire in some measure to understand thy truth, which my heart believes and loves. For I do not seek to understand in order to believe, but I believe in order to understand. For this too I believe, that "unless I believe, I shall not understand" [Isa. 7:9, Old Latin version quoted by Augustine].

Chapter 2. And so, O Lord, since thou givest understanding to faith, give me to understand—as far as thou knowest it to be good for me—that thou dost exist, as we believe, and that thou art what we believe thee to be. Now we believe that thou art a being than which none greater can be thought. Or can it be that there is no such being, since "the fool hath said in his heart, 'There is no God'" [Ps.

14:1]? But when this same fool hears what I am saying—"A being than which none greater can be thought"—he understands what he hears, and what he understands is in his understanding, even if he does not understand that it exists. For it is one thing for an object to be in the understanding, and another thing to understand that it exists. When a painter considers beforehand what he is going to paint, he has it in his understanding, but he does not suppose that what he has not yet painted already exists. But when he has painted it, he both has it in his understanding and understands that what he has now produced exists. Even the fool, then, must be convinced that a being than which none greater can be thought exists at least in his understanding, since when he hears this he understands it, and whatever is understood is in the understanding. But clearly that than which a greater cannot be thought cannot exist in the understanding alone. For if it is actually in the understanding alone, it can be thought of as existing also in reality, and this is greater. Therefore, if that than which a greater cannot be thought is in the understanding alone, this same thing than which a greater cannot be thought is that than which a greater can be thought. But obviously this is impossible. Without doubt, therefore, there exists, both in the understanding and in reality, something than which a greater cannot be thought.

Chapter 3.   And certainly it exists so truly that it cannot be thought of as nonexistent. For something can be thought of as existing, which cannot be thought of as not existing, and this is greater than that which *can* be thought of as not existing. Thus, if that than which a greater cannot be thought can be thought of as not existing, this very thing than which a greater cannot be thought is *not* that than which a greater cannot be thought. But this is contradictory. So, then, there truly is a being than which a greater cannot be thought—so truly that it cannot even be thought of as not existing.

And *thou* art this being, O Lord our God. Thou so truly art, then, O Lord my God, that thou canst not even be thought of as not existing. And this is right. For if some mind could think of something better than thou, the creature would rise above the Creator and judge its Creator; but this is altogether absurd. And indeed, whatever is, except thyself alone, can be thought of as not existing. Thou alone, therefore, of all beings, hast being in the truest and highest sense, since no other being so truly exists, and thus every other being has less being. Why, then, has "the fool said in his heart, 'There is no

God,' " when it is so obvious to the rational mind that, of all beings, thou dost exist supremely? Why indeed, unless it is that he is a stupid fool?

From *A Scholastic Miscellany: Anselm to Ockham,* edited and translated by Eugene R. Fairweather (Volume X: The Library of Christian Classics), pages 73–75. First published in MCMLVI by the SCM Press Ltd., London, and The Westminster Press, Philadelphia. Used by permission of the publishers.

Anselm of Canterbury

From *Why God Became Man*

In the early Middle Ages the view found in Irenaeus, Gregory of Nyssa, and Augustine that Christ saves us by defeating the devil and freeing us from his power seems to have dominated theorizing about the atonement. Anselm rejected it. He could not accept the assumption that the devil could ever have had legitimate power over us and needed to be bargained with or defeated. In this treatise Anselm developed his own account, applying reason boldly to the analysis of faith. After some introductory material, the work takes the form of a dialogue between Anselm and his student Boso.

Preface. I have been compelled to finish the following work as best I could, more hastily than I found convenient, and therefore more briefly than I wished. . . . I have named it *Why God Became Man,* from the theme on which it was written, and I have divided it into two short books. The first of these contains the objections of unbelievers who reject the Christian faith because they regard it as contrary to reason, along with the answers of believers. It ends by proving by necessary reasons (Christ being put out of sight, as if nothing had ever been known of him) that it is impossible for any man to be saved without him. . . . .

Book 1

Chapter 1. . . . I am told that these proofs are thought to be both pleasing and adequate. Those who make this request do not expect to come to faith through reason, but they hope to be gladdened by the understanding and contemplation of the things they believe, and as far as possible to be "ready always to satisfy every one that asketh" them "a reason of that hope which is in" them [1 Peter 3:15]. . . .

Chapter 11. . . . *Anselm:* If an angel or a man always rendered to God what is due to him, he would never sin.

Boso: I cannot contradict you.

A: Thus to sin is the same thing as not to render his due to God.

B: What is the debt which we owe to God?

A: Every inclination of the rational creature ought to be subject to the will of God.

B: Nothing could be truer.

A: This is the debt which angels and men owe to God. No one who pays it sins; everyone who does not pay it sins. This is the justice or rectitude of the will, which makes men just or upright in heart, that is, in will. This is the whole and entire honor which we owe to God, and God requires from us. . . . So, then, everyone who sins must repay to God the honor that he has taken away, and this is the satisfaction that every sinner ought to make to God. . . .

Chapter 12. . . . *Anselm:* Let us go back and see whether it is fitting for God to remit sins by mercy alone, without any payment for the honor taken away from him.

Boso: I do not see why it is not fitting.

A: To remit sin in this way is the same thing as not to punish it. And since to deal rightly with sin without satisfaction is the same thing as to punish it, if it is not punished it is remitted irregularly.

B: What you say is reasonable.

A: But it is not fitting for God to remit any irregularity in his Kingdom.

B: I am afraid of sinning, if I want to say anything different.

A: Then it is not fitting for God to remit sin thus unpunished.

B: That follows. . . .

Chapter 19. . . . *Anselm:* Then hold it as most certain that without satisfaction, that is, without the willing payment of man's debt, God cannot remit sin unpunished, any more than the sinner can attain even to such blessedness as he had before he sinned. . . .

Chapter 25. Boso: How, then, will man be saved if he himself does not pay what he owes and he ought not to be saved unless he pays it? Or with what shame shall we declare that God, who is rich in mercy beyond man's understanding, cannot do this work of mercy? . . .

A: Do you not understand from what we have said before that some men must attain to blessedness? It is true that it is unfitting for God to bring man with any stain on him to the end for which he made him without any stain, lest he seem either to regret his good undertaking or to be unable to carry out his plan. But, on account of the same incongruity, it is much more impossible that no man at all should be raised to the end for which he was created. Therefore, some such satisfaction for sin, as we have already shown to be necessary, must be found. . . .

Book 2

Chapter 6. Anselm: But this cannot be done unless there is some-one to pay to God for human sin something greater than everything that exists, except God.

Boso: So it is agreed.

A: If he is to give something of his own to God, which surpasses everything that is beneath God, it is also necessary for him to be greater than everything that is not God.

B: I cannot deny it.

A: But there is nothing above everything that is not God, save God himself.

B: That is true.

A: Then no one but God can make this satisfaction.

B: That follows.

A: But no one ought to make it except man; otherwise man does not make satisfaction.

B: Nothing seems more just.

A: If then, as is certain, that celestial city must be completed from among men, and this cannot happen unless the aforesaid satisfaction is made, while no one save God can make it and no one save man ought to make it, it is necessary for a God-Man to make it.

From *A Scholastic Miscellany: Anselm to Ockham,* edited and translated by Eugene R. Fairweather (Volume X: The Library of Christian Classics), pages 100–101, 119–120, 135, 144–145, 150–151. First published in MCMLVI by the SCM Press Ltd., London, and The Westminster Press, Philadelphia. Used by permission of the publishers.

Peter Abelard (1079–1142)

From *Exposition of the Epistle to the Romans*

Whether one agreed with him or not, Abelard had a way of dominating the scene. He became the most famous teacher at the University of Paris, fell in love with the wise and beautiful Héloïse, married her in secret, was seized and castrated by her angry guardian, and retired to a monastery. In his famous Yes and No, *he collected passages from the Bible and earlier theologians on both sides of important theological issues. He said he sought only clarifying debate, but the juxtaposition of apparent contradictions suggests an impish love of controversy. Yet, as this passage implicitly taking issue with Anselm suggests, he was a serious philosopher and theologian.*

In what way does the apostle declare that we are justified or reconciled to God through the death of his Son, when God ought to have been the more angered against man, inasmuch as men acted more criminally by crucifying his Son than they ever did by transgressing his first command in paradise through the tasting of a single apple? For the more men's sins were multiplied, the more just it would have been for God to be angry with men. And if that sin of Adam was so great that it could be expiated only by the death of Christ, what expiation will avail for that act of murder committed against Christ, and for the many great crimes committed against him or his followers? How did the death of his innocent Son so please God the Father that through it he should be reconciled to us—to us who by our sinful acts have done the very things for which our innocent Lord was put to death? Had not this very great sin been committed, could he not have pardoned the former much lighter sin? Had not evil deeds been multiplied, could he not have done such a good thing for man?

In what manner have we been made more righteous through the death of the Son of God than we were before, so that we ought to be delivered from punishment? . . . Indeed, how cruel and wicked it seems that anyone should demand the blood of an innocent person as the price for anything, or that it should in any way please him that an innocent man should be slain—still less that God should consider the death of his Son so agreeable that by it he should be reconciled to the whole world! . . .

Now it seems to us that we have been justified by the blood of Christ and reconciled to God in this way: through his unique act of grace manifested to us—in that his Son has taken upon himself our nature and persevered therein in teaching us by word and example even unto death—he has more fully found us to himself by love; with the result that our hearts should be enkindled by such a gift of divine grace, and true charity should not now shrink from enduring anything for him.

And we do not doubt that the ancient Fathers, waiting in faith for this same gift, were aroused to very great love of God in the same way as men of this dispensation of grace, since it is written: "And they that went before and they that followed cried, saying: 'Hosanna to the Son of David,' " etc. [Mark 11:9; 21:9]. Yet everyone becomes more righteous—by which we mean a greater lover of the Lord—after the Passion of Christ than before, since a realized gift inspires greater love than one which is only hoped for. Wherefore, our redemption through Christ's suffering is that deeper affection in us which not only frees us from slavery to sin, but also wins for us the true liberty of sons of God, so that we do all things out of love rather than fear—love to him who has shown us such grace that no greater can be found, as he himself asserts, saying, "Greater love than this no man hath, that a man lay down his life for his friends" [John 15:13]. Of this love the Lord says elsewhere, "I am come to cast fire on the earth, and what will I, but that it blaze forth?" [Luke 12:49]. So does he bear witness that he came for the express purpose of spreading this true liberty of love amongst men.

From *A Scholastic Miscellany: Anselm to Ockham,* translated by Gerald E. Moffatt (Volume X: The Library of Christian Classics), pages 282–284. First published in MCMLVI by the SCM Press Ltd., London, and The Westminster Press, Philadelphia. Used by permission of the publishers.

Francis of Assisi (c.1182–1226)

The Canticle of Brother Sun

As a young man, Francis gave all his possessions to the poor and set off on a wandering life of preaching and prayer and poverty. He soon attracted followers, and Pope Innocent III approved the founding of

this new order of poor brothers. Francis wrote this famous poem, in ill
health, in the last year of his life.

Most High, all-powerful, good Lord,
Yours are the praises, the glory, the honor, and all blessing.
To You alone, Most High, do they belong,
and no man is worthy to mention Your name.
Praised be You, my Lord, with all your creatures,
especially Sir Brother Sun,
Who is the day and through whom You give us light.
And he is beautiful and radiant with great splendor;
and bears a likeness of You, Most High One.
Praised be You, my Lord, through Sister Moon and the stars,
in heaven You formed them clear and precious and beautiful.
Praised be You, my Lord, through Brother Wind,
and through the air, cloudy and serene, and every kind of weather
through which You give sustenance to Your creatures.
Praised be You, my Lord, through Sister Water,
which is very useful and humble and precious and chaste.
Praised be You, my Lord, through Brother Fire,
through whom You light the night
and he is beautiful and playful and robust and strong.
Praised be You, my Lord, through our Sister Mother Earth,
who sustains and governs us,
and who produces varied fruits with colored flowers and herbs.
Praised be You, my Lord, through those who give pardon for Your
    love
and bear infirmity and tribulation.
Blessed are those who endure in peace
for by You, Most High, they shall be crowned.
Praised be You, my Lord, through our Sister Bodily Death,
from whom no living man can escape.
Woe to those who die in mortal sin.
Blessed are those whom death will find in Your most holy will,
for the second death shall do them no harm.
Praise and bless my Lord and give Him thanks
and serve him with great humility.

Francis of Assisi

From *The Testament*

Francis dictated this testament to his brothers shortly before he died. Already the original Franciscan commitment to absolute poverty was under challenge from high authorities, and Francis was here obviously urging his followers to faithfulness to the church hierarchy—though not without a critical spirit.

The Lord granted me, Brother Francis, to begin to do penance in this way: While I was in sin, it seemed very bitter to me to see lepers. And the Lord Himself led me among them and I had mercy upon them. And when I left them that which seemed bitter to me was changed into sweetness of soul and body; and afterward I lingered a little and left the world. . . .

Afterward the Lord gave me and still gives me such faith in priests who live according to the manner of the holy Roman Church because of their order, that if they were to persecute me, I would [still] have recourse to them. . . . And I do not wish to consider sin in them because I discern the Son of God in them and they are my masters. And I act in this way since I see nothing corporally of the Most High Son of God in this world except His Most holy Body and Blood which they receive and which they alone administer to others. . . .

And after the Lord gave me brothers, no one showed me what I should do, but the Most High Himself revealed to me that I should live according to the form of the Holy Gospel. And I had this written down simply and in a few words and the Lord Pope confirmed it for me. And those who came to receive life gave to the poor everything which they were capable of possessing and they were content with one tunic, patched inside and out, with a cord and short trousers. And we had no desire for anything more. . . .

And whoever shall have observed these [things], may he be filled in heaven with the blessing of the most high Father and on earth with the blessing of His beloved Son with the most Holy Spirit the Paraclete and with all the powers of heaven and all the saints. And I, little brother Francis, your servant, inasmuch as I can, confirm for you this most holy blessing both within and without.

Bonaventure (c.1217–1274)

From *Retracing the Arts to Theology*

Bonaventure was a Franciscan, a mystic, a professor at the University of Paris, and eventually head of the Franciscan order and author of the official biography of Francis. He was a theologian of great intellectual sophistication, but in the face of Aquinas' efforts to distinguish the realms of faith and reason, Bonaventure remained in the tradition of Augustine and Anselm, in which all knowing begins with faith. He probably wrote this essay in the early 1250s, as a colleague of Aquinas on the faculty at Paris.

1. *"Every best gift and every perfect gift is from above, coming down from the Father of lights,"* James in the first chapter of his Epistle. These words of Sacred Scripture not only reveal the source of all illumination but they likewise point out the generous flow of manifold rays which issue from that Fount of light. Notwithstanding the fact that every illumination of knowledge is within, still, we can with propriety distinguish what we may call the *external* light, or the light of mechanical skill; the *lower* light, or the light of sense perception; the *inner* light, or the light of philosophical knowledge; and the *higher* light, or the light of grace and of Sacred Scripture. The first light illumines in the consideration of the *arts and crafts;* the second, in regard to *natural form;* the third, in regard to *intellectual truth;* the fourth and last, in regard to *saving truth.* . . .

8. Let us see, therefore, how the other illuminations of knowledge are to be reduced to the light of Sacred Scripture. First of all, let us consider the illumination of *sense* perception, which is concerned exclusively with the cognition of sensible objects. . . . If we consider the *medium* of perception, we shall see therein the Word begotten from all eternity and made man in time. Indeed, a sensible object can make an impression upon a cognitive faculty only through the medium of a likeness which proceeds from the object as an offspring from its parent, and in every sensation, this likeness must be present. . . . In like manner, know that from the mind of the Most High, Who

is knowable by the interior senses of the mind, from all eternity there emanated a Likeness, an Image, and an Offspring; and afterwards, when "the fulness of time had come" He was united to a mind and body and assumed the form of man which He had never been before, and through Him all our minds, which bear the likeness of the Father through faith in our hearts, are brought back to God. . . .

11. By the same process of reasoning is Divine Wisdom to be found in the illumination of the mechanical arts, the sole purpose of which is the *production of works of art.* . . .

12. If we consider the *production,* we shall see that the work of art proceeds from the artificer according to a model existing in his mind; this pattern or model the artificer studies carefully before he produces and then he produces as he has predetermined. The artificer, moreover, produces an exterior work bearing the closest possible resemblance to the interior model, and if it were in his power to produce an effect which would know and love him, this he would assuredly do; and if that creature could know its maker, it would be by means of a likeness according to which it came from the hands of the artificer. . . . In like manner, understand that no creature has proceeded from the Most High Creator except through the Eternal Word, "in Whom He ordered all things," and by which Word He produced creatures bearing not only the nature of His *vestige* but also of His *image* so that through knowledge and love, they might be united to Him. And since by sin the rational creature had dimmed the eye of contemplation, it was most fitting that the Eternal and Invisible should become visible and take flesh that He might lead us back to the Father. . . .

15. In the same way is Divine Wisdom to be found in the illumination of *rational philosophy,* the main purpose of which is concerned with *speech.* . . .

16. Considering speech in the light of the *speaker,* we see that all speech is the expression of a *mental concept.* That inner concept is the word of the mind and its offspring which is known to the person conceiving it, but that it may become known to the hearer, it assumes the nature of the voice and clothed in that form, the intelligible word becomes sensible and is heard without; it is received into the ear of the person listening and, still, it does not depart from the mind of the person uttering it. Practically the same procedure is seen in the begetting of the Eternal Word, because the Father conceived Him, begetting Him from all eternity. . . . But that He might be known by man who is endowed with senses, He assumed the nature of flesh,

and "the Word was made flesh and dwelt amongst us," and yet He remained "in the bosom of His Father." . . .

26. And thus it is clear how the *manifold Wisdom of God,* which is clearly revealed in Sacred Scripture, lies hidden in all knowledge and in all nature. It is clear also how all divisions of knowledge are handmaids of theology. It is likewise evident how wide is the luminous way and how in everything which is perceived or known, God Himself lies hidden within.

From *Saint Bonaventure's De Reductione Artium ad Theologiam,* a Commentary with an Introduction and Translation by Emma Thérèse Healy (Saint Bonaventure, N.Y.: The Franciscan Institute, Saint Bonaventure University, 1955). Copyright, 1940, by Sister Emma Thérèse Healy. Used by permission of the Sisters of St. Joseph.

Thomas Aquinas (c.1224–1274)

From *Summa Theologiae*

Aquinas was born in Italy, fled his disapproving family to join the Dominicans, taught in Paris, and returned to Italy to advise the pope and teach at the University of Naples. His Summa Theologiae *is one of the monuments of the Middle Ages; it balances the claims of faith and reason, nature and grace. While Aquinas is now the most honored of Catholic theologians, he was distinctly controversial in his own lifetime—a Dominican at a university where the friars were unwelcome, an Aristotelian in a time when Aristotle seemed intellectually dangerous. Some of his teachings were even condemned shortly after his death. The* Summa *takes a form characteristic of medieval analyses: Thomas first presents arguments or authorities against his position, then cites an authority in support of his view, states his own position, and finally answers objections.*

Part 1

Question 1. Article 1. Whether another doctrine is necessary, besides the philosophical sciences.

We proceed to the first article thus:

1. It seems that there is no need for any other doctrine besides the philosophical sciences. Man should not strive to know what is above reason, since it is said in Ecclesiasticus 3:22: "seek not to know what

is higher than thyself." Now what is within the reach of reason is adequately dealt with in the philosophical sciences. It seems superfluous, therefore, that there should be another doctrine besides the philosophical sciences. . . .

On the other hand: it is said in 2 Tim. 3:16: "All scripture is given by inspiration of God, and is profitable for doctrine, for correction, for instruction in righteousness." Now the divinely inspired Scriptures are quite distinct from the philosophical sciences, which are devised by human reason. It is therefore expedient that there should be another science which is divinely inspired, besides the philosophical sciences.

I answer: it was necessary for man's salvation that there should be a doctrine founded on revelation, as well as the philosophical sciences discovered by human reason. It was necessary, in the first place, because man is ordained to God as his end, who surpasses the comprehension of reason, according to Isa. 64:4: "neither hath the eye seen, O God, besides thee, what he has prepared for him that waiteth for him." Men must have some foreknowledge of the end to which they ought to direct their intentions and actions. It was therefore necessary that some things which transcend human reason should be made known through divine revelation. It was necessary also that man should be instructed by divine revelation even in such things concerning God as human reason could discover. For such truth about God as could be discovered by reason would be known only by the few, and that after a long time, and mixed with many errors. Now the whole salvation of man, which lies in God, depends on knowledge of this truth. It was therefore necessary that men should be instructed in divine things through divine revelation, in order that their salvation might come to pass the more fittingly and certainly. It was necessary, therefore, that there should be a sacred doctrine given through revelation, as well as the philosophical sciences discovered by reason. . . .

Question 2. Article 3. Whether God exists. . . .

1. It seems that God does not exist. If one of two contraries were to be infinite, the other would be wholly excluded. Now the name "God" means that he is infinite good. There would therefore be no evil if God were to exist. But there is evil in the world. It follows that God does not exist.

2. Again, what can be explained by comparatively few principles is not the consequence of a greater number of principles. Now if we

suppose that God does not exist, it appears that we can still account for all that we see in the world by other principles, attributing all natural things to nature as their principle, and all that is purposive to human reason or will. There is therefore no need to suppose that God exists.

On the other hand: in Ex. 3:14 God says in person: "I AM THAT I AM."

I answer: God's existence can be proved in five ways. The first and clearest proof is the argument from motion. It is certain, and in accordance with sense experience, that some things in this world are moved. Now everything that is moved is moved by something else, since nothing is moved unless it is potentially that to which it is moved, whereas that which moves is actual. To move is nothing other than to bring something from potentiality to actuality, and a thing can be brought from potentiality to actuality only by something which is actual. Thus a fire, which is actually hot, makes wood, which is potentially hot, to be actually hot, so moving and altering it. Now it is impossible for the same thing to be both actual and potential in the same respect, although it may be so in different respects. What is actually hot cannot at the same time be potentially hot, although it is potentially cold. It is therefore impossible that, in the same respect and in the same way, anything should be both mover and moved, or that it should move itself. Whatever is moved must therefore be moved by something else. If, then, that by which it is moved is itself moved, this also must be moved by something else, and this in turn by something else again. But this cannot go on for ever, since there would then be no first mover, and consequently no other mover, because secondary movers cannot move unless moved by a first mover, as a staff cannot move unless it is moved by the hand. We are therefore bound to arrive at a first mover which is not moved by anything, and all men understand that this is God.

The second way is from the nature of an efficient cause. We find that there is a sequence of efficient causes in sensible things. But we do not find that anything is the efficient cause of itself. Nor is this possible, for the thing would then be prior to itself, which is impossible. But neither can the sequence of efficient causes be infinite, for in every sequence the first efficient cause is the cause of an intermediate cause, and an intermediate cause is the cause of the ultimate cause, whether the intermediate causes be many, or only one. Now if a cause is removed, its effect is removed. Hence if there were no first efficient cause, there would be no ultimate cause, and no intermediate cause. But if the regress of efficient causes were infinite, there would be no first efficient cause. There would consequently be no ultimate effect, and no intermediate causes. But this is plainly false. We are therefore bound to suppose that there is a first efficient cause. And all men call this God.

The third way is from the nature of possibility and necessity. There are some things which may either exist or not exist, since some things come to be and pass away, and may therefore be or not be. Now it is impossible that all of these should exist at all times, because there is at least some time when that which may possibly not exist does not exist. Hence if all things were such that they might not exist, at some time or other there would be nothing. But if this were true there would be nothing existing now, since what does not exist cannot begin to exist, unless through something which does exist. If there had been nothing existing, it would have been impossible for anything to begin to exist, and there would now be nothing at all. But this is plainly false, and hence not all existence is merely possible. Something in things must be necessary. Now everything which is necessary either derives its necessity from elsewhere, or does not. But we cannot go on to infinity with necessary things which have a cause of their necessity, any more than with efficient causes, as we proved. We are therefore bound to suppose something necessary in itself, which does not owe its necessity to anything else, but which is the cause of the necessity of other things. And all men call this God.

The fourth way is from the degrees that occur in things, which are found to be more and less good, true, noble, and so on. Things are said to be more and less because they approximate in different degrees to that which is greatest. A thing is the more hot the more it approximates to that which is hottest. There is therefore something which is the truest, the best, and the noblest, and which is consequently the greatest in being, since that which has the greatest truth is also greatest in being, as is said in 2 *Metaphysics,* text 4.* Now that which most thoroughly possesses the nature of any genus is the cause of all that the genus contains. Thus fire, which is most perfectly hot, is the cause of all hot things, as is said in the same passage. There is therefore something which is the cause of the being of all things that are, as well as of their goodness and their every perfection. This we call God.

---

*As he does so often, Aquinas is referring to Aristotle.

The fifth way is from the governance of things. We see how some things, like natural bodies, work for an end even though they have no knowledge. The fact that they nearly always operate in the same way, and so as to achieve the maximum good, makes this obvious, and shows that they attain their end by design, not by chance. Now things which have no knowledge tend towards an end only through the agency of something which knows and also understands, as an arrow through an archer. There is therefore an intelligent being by whom all natural things are directed to their end. This we call God.

On the first point: as Augustine says [*Enchiridion* 11]: "since God is supremely good, he would not allow any evil thing to exist in his works, were he not able by his omnipotence and goodness to bring good out of evil." God's infinite goodness is such that he permits evil things to exist, and brings good out of them.

On the second point: everything that can be attributed to nature must depend on God as its first cause, since nature works for a predetermined end through the direction of a higher agent. Similarly, whatever is due to purpose must depend on a cause higher than the reason or will of man, since these are subject to change and defect. Anything which is changeable and subject to defect must depend on some first principle which is immovable and necessary in itself, as we have shown. . . .

Question 23. Article 1. Whether men are predestined by God. . . .

I answer: it is rightly said that God predestines men. We have shown that all things are ruled by divine providence, and that providence ordains things to their end. Now the end to which God ordains creatures is twofold. There is, first, the end which exceeds the proportion and the capacity of created nature. This is eternal life, which consists in the vision of the divine essence, which is beyond the nature of any creature. . . . There is, secondly, the end which is proportionate to created nature, which a created thing may attain by means of its own natural power. Now when a thing cannot attain something by its own natural power, it must be directed to it by another, as an arrow is directed to its mark by an archer. Properly speaking, then, although a rational creature is capable of eternal life, he is brought to this life by God. The reason why he is brought to eternal life must therefore pre-exist in God, since the reason why anything is ordained to its end lies in God, and we have said that this is providence. The reason which exists in the mind of an agent is, as it were, a pre-existence in him of the thing which he intends to do.

We give the name of "predestination" to the reason why a rational creature is brought to eternal life, because to destine means to bring. It is plain, then, that predestination is a part of providence, if we consider it in relation to its objects. . . .

Part 1 of Part 2

Question 85. Article 2. Whether the whole good of human nature can be destroyed by sin. . . .

I answer: we said in the preceding article that the natural good which sin diminishes is the natural inclination to virtue. Now the reason why man inclines to virtue is that he is rational. It is because he is rational that he acts in accordance with reason, and this is to act virtuously. But a man would not be able to sin without his rational nature. Sin cannot then deprive him of it altogether. It follows that his inclination to virtue cannot be entirely destroyed. . . .

Question 109. Article 2. Whether a man can will or do good without grace. . . .

I answer: man's nature may be considered in two ways, either in its purity, as it was in our first parent before sin, or as corrupt, as it is in ourselves after the sin of our first parent. In either state, human nature needs divine help in order to do or to will any good, since it needs a first mover, as we said in the preceding article. In regard to the sufficiency of his operative power, man in the state of pure nature could will and do, by his own natural power, the good proportionate to his nature. . . . In the state of corrupt nature he falls short of what nature makes possible, so that he cannot by his own power fulfil the whole good that pertains to his nature. Human nature is not so entirely corrupted by sin, however, as to be deprived of natural good altogether. Consequently, even in the state of corrupt nature a man can do some particular good by the power of his own nature, such as build houses, plant vineyards, and things of this kind. But he cannot achieve the whole good natural to him, as if he lacked nothing. One who is infirm, similarly, can make some movements by himself, but cannot move himself naturally like a man in health, unless cured by the help of medicine.

Thus in the state of pure nature man needs a power added to his natural power by grace, for one reason, namely, in order to do and to will supernatural good. But in the state of corrupt nature he needs this for two reasons, in order to be healed, and in order to achieve the meritorious good of supernatural virtue. In both states, moreover, he needs the divine help by which he is moved to act well. . . .

Question 114. Article 1. Whether a man can merit anything from God. . . .

I answer: merit and reward mean the same thing. We call it a reward when it is given to someone in return for his work or labor, as a price for it. Now to give a reward for work or labor is an act of justice. . . . Justice obtains absolutely between those between whom equality obtains absolutely. It does not obtain absolutely between those between whom equality does not obtain absolutely, but there may nevertheless be a kind of justice between them, since we speak of the "right" of a father, or of a master. . . .

Now there is obviously a very great inequality between God and man. The gulf betwixt them is indeed infinite. Moreover, all the good that is in a man is due to God. The kind of justice which obtains where there is absolute equality cannot therefore obtain between man and God. There obtains only the justice which is relative to the proportion of what is wrought by each, according to their own mode. But since both the mode and the manner of man's virtue are due to God, it is only by a previous divine ordination that a man can merit anything from God. That is, a man can receive as a reward from God only what God has given him the power to work for by his own effort; just as natural things attain, by their own movements and activities, that to which they are divinely ordained. There is this difference, however. A rational creature moves itself to its action by its free will, and its action is therefore meritorious. This is not the case with other creatures.

From *Aquinas on Nature and Grace,* translated and edited by A. M. Fairweather (Volume XI: The Library of Christian Classics), pages 35–36, 53–56, 102, 128, 140–141, 203–204. First published in MCMLIV by the SCM Press Ltd., London, and The Westminster Press, Philadelphia. Used by permission of the publishers.

Part 3

Question 1. Article 2. Whether it was necessary for the restoration of the human race that the word of God should become incarnate. . . .

I answer that, A thing is said to be necessary for a certain end in two ways. First, when the end cannot be without it; as food is necessary for the preservation of human life. Secondly, when the end is attained better and more conveniently, as a horse is necessary for a journey. In the first way it was not necessary that God should become incarnate for the restoration of human nature. For God in His omnipotent power could have restored human nature in many other ways. But in the second way it was necessary that God should become incarnate for the restoration of human nature. Hence Augustine says: "We shall also show that other ways were not wanting to God, to Whose power all things are equally subject; but that there was not a more fitting way of healing our misery" [*On the Trinity* 13.10].

Now this may be viewed with respect to our *furtherance in good.* First, with regard to faith, which is made more certain by believing God Himself Who speaks; hence Augustine says: "In order that man might journey more trustfully toward the truth, the Truth itself, the Son of God, having assumed human nature, established and founded faith" [*The City of God* 11.2]. Secondly, with regard to hope, which is thereby greatly strengthened; hence Augustine says: "Nothing was so necessary for raising our hope as to show us how deeply God loved us. And what could afford us a stronger proof of this than that the Son of God should become a partner with us of human nature?" [*On the Trinity* 13.10]. Thirdly, with regard to charity, which is greatly enkindled by this; hence Augustine says: "What greater cause is there of the Lord's coming than to show God's love for us?" [*De Catech. Rudib.* 4]. And he afterwards adds: "If we have been slow to love, at least let us hasten to love in return." Fourthly, with regard to well-doing, in which He set us an example; hence Augustine says in a sermon: "Man who might be seen was not to be followed; but God was to be followed, Who could not be seen. And therefore God was made man, that He Who might be seen by man, and Whom man might follow, might be shown to man" [*Ser.* 22, *On Temptation*]. Fifthly, with regard to the full participation of the Divinity, which is the true bliss of man and end of human life; and this is bestowed upon us by Christ's humanity; for Augustine says in a sermon: "God was made man, that man might be made God" [*Ser.* 13, *On Temptation*].

So also was this useful for our *withdrawal from evil.* First, because man is taught by it not to prefer the devil to himself, nor to honor him who is the author of sin; hence Augustine says: "Since human nature is so united to God as to become one person, let not these proud spirits dare to prefer themselves to man, because they have no bodies" [*On the Trinity* 13.17]. Secondly, because we are thereby taught how great is man's dignity, lest we should sully it with sin; hence Augustine says: "God has proved to us how high a place human nature holds amongst creatures, inasmuch as He appeared to men as a true man" [*On True Religion* 16]. And Pope Leo says in a sermon on the Nativity: "Learn, O Christian, thy worth; and being made a partner of the Divine nature, refuse to return by evil deeds to your former worthlessness [21]. Thirdly, because, "in order to do away with man's presumption, the grace of God is commended to us in Jesus Christ, though no merits of ours went before," as Augustine says [*On the Trinity* 13.17]. Fourthly, because "man's pride, which is the greatest stumbling block to our clinging to God, can be convinced and cured by humility so great," as Augustine says in the same place. Fifthly, in order to free man from the thraldom of sin, which, as Augustine says, "ought to be done in such a way that the devil should be overcome by the justice of the man Jesus Christ" [*On the Trinity* 13.13], and this was done by Christ satisfying for us. Now a mere man could not have satisfied for the whole human race, and God was not bound to satisfy; hence it behooved Jesus Christ to be both God and man. Hence Pope Leo says in the same sermon: "Weakness is assumed by strength, lowliness by majesty, mortality by eternity, in order that one and the same Mediator of God and men might die in one and rise in the other—for this was our fitting remedy. Unless He was God, He would not have brought a remedy; and unless He was man, He would not have set an example."

From Thomas Aquinas, *Summa Theologica,* Volume 2, translated by Fathers of the English Dominican Province, page 2027. Copyright © 1947 by Benzinger Brothers. Used by permission of Glencoe Publishing Company.

Giles of Rome (c.1245–1316)

From *On Ecclesiastical Power*

Giles was born in Italy but moved to France. There he studied under Aquinas at Paris, though in this treatise he diverged from Aquinas' position by defending the absolute power of the Papacy so forcefully that he leaves secular authorities no real independence.

Book 2

Chapter 6. In various chapters of this short work we have tried to state more clearly how earthly power, because it rules over temporal matters, is rightly and properly subject to the spiritual power, so that from this we may be able to infer that the spiritual power rules not only over the temporal power but also over temporal matters, inasmuch as the ecclesiastical authority is shown to have dominion over both temporal matters and their rulers. . . .

Now we see that natural causes have the capacity to act by means of natural powers; fire, for example, can heat by means of heat and of the heating power that it possesses, and water can cool by means of its cooling power, and the heaven by means of its power can affect the things here below. Each natural thing, then, has the capacity to act by virtue of its power and its potency. And just as natural causes are capable of acting by virtue of natural powers, so artists are capable of acting by means of the arts. Thus the lute player can play the lute properly by virtue of the art of lute-playing, whereas the man who lacks this art cannot do so. Thirdly, wise men are capable of exercising their activity by means of the sciences. Thus one becomes capable of knowing the parts and properties of mobile bodies by means of natural philosophy, and one becomes capable of contemplating and knowing what is explained in the other sciences by means of these sciences. Finally, rulers are capable of acting by means of the ruling powers, whether these ruling powers be material or spiritual; and so each one enjoys his own right and rules in virtue of his own ruling power.

Thus we have distinguished four kinds of powers: one kind is the natural powers, another is the arts, a third the sciences, and a fourth the powers by which men are ruled and governed. . . .

Thus we see that among the natural powers some are higher and others lower. The heavenly powers, for example, are higher than those of the elements, inasmuch as the powers of the elements do not act except by the power of the heaven; for, as natural philosophy teaches, fire does not or could not generate fire save by the power of the heaven. . . . Therefore, the heavenly power, being more common and universal, dominates all the other powers, whether they be those of the elements or those of the compounds of elements.

Just as in natural things we see that some powers are higher and others lower, so too in the arts some are higher and others lower; for instance, there is an art of bridle-making and there is likewise an art that consists in knowing how to make use of an army; and these two arts are not to be regarded as equals. Rather one is subordinated to the other: the art of bridle-making is subordinated to the art of warfare and thus makes such bridles as are useful to the soldier. . . .

Thus we have indicated the reasons and causes for which in nature and in the arts one agent serves another. As to the sciences, we can indicate a third reason and cause for which one serves the other: each one of the sciences discovered by the human mind serves metaphysics not only because metaphysics is more general and more universal than the other sciences but also because it attains what is best more perfectly. Indeed, among the sciences discovered by the human mind, metaphysics is able to study God, who is the most perfect of beings, better than any other science. And hence, since theology attains what is best more perfectly than metaphysics and any particular science, it is the queen of the sciences and engages all the sciences in its service, so that metaphysics itself is its handmaiden and servant. . . .

As to the fourth kind of power, namely, ruling and governing, we shall say that all three causes concur simultaneously. For we shall say that earthly power and rule must obey and serve the spiritual power and rule for all three reasons mentioned: because it is more particular, and because it disposes and prepares the materials, and because this earthly power does not come so close to what is best or attain it so perfectly as the other.

Now ecclesiastical power is more universal than earthly power because the church is said to be catholic, that is, universal . . . for . . . "catholic" is the Greek term for universal. If then it is an article of faith that we must believe in the Holy Catholic Church, he is not a true believer who does not believe the church to be catholic—that is, universal. . . .

Now all the other rules are particular because there is not a single one that is indispensable to the attainment of salvation, and this is especially true of secular rules and earthly powers, inasmuch as one draws nearer to salvation by disengaging himself from them. Indeed, clerics, who are not subject to earthly power, are in a more perfect state than laymen, who are subject to it. . . . Therefore the church should rule throughout the entire world and all men should be subject to it, since if they are not, they will find the gates of heaven shut and so will not be able to enter the kingdom of heaven. . . .

Secondly, earthly power will be subordinated to ecclesiastical power as the one who prepares the materials is subordinated to the one for whom he prepares them. For it pertains to earthly power through the church and under its authority to receive the material sword and to rule over temporal and material affairs and even over the bodies of men, as far as laymen and the affairs over which they have been granted power are concerned.

It will be the duty of earthly power, therefore, to administer justice in these matters, so that no one may wrong anyone else in his body or in his affairs and so that every citizen and every believer may fare well. Thus the duty of earthly power is to prepare the materials in order that the ecclesiastical ruler may not be hampered in spiritual matters. For the body was made to serve the soul, and temporal goods to serve the body. . . . Hence, just as bridle-making equips a horse with a bridle and prepares the horse to serve the soldier more readily, so earthly power puts a bridle on the laymen, lest they interfere with the church or with one another, and disposes them to submit more readily to ecclesiastical power. . . .

Thirdly, earthly power is subordinate to ecclesiastical power as that which attains what is best is subordinate to that which attains it more perfectly. We observe this mode of subordination in the sciences; for example, metaphysics, which treats of God, is the goddess of the sciences discovered by man, and all the other human sciences are subordinated to it and serve it and are directed by it. According to this mode, ecclesiastical power, which is spiritual and which deals with the things that pertain to God, is the mistress of earthly power; and it belongs to it to direct this earthly power, and earthly power must be subject to the rule of the priest.

Translated by Joseph Sheerin. Reprinted with permission of The Free Press, a Division of Macmillan, Inc., from *Medieval Political Philosophy,* edited by Ralph Lerner and Mushin Mahdi, pages 392–401. Copyright © 1963 by The Free Press.

Dante Alighieri (1265–1321)

From *De Monarchia*

Dante is best known as the author of the incomparable Divine Comedy, *but his interests and abilities ranged very widely indeed. In a time when supporters of pope and emperor were tearing Italy apart, Dante argued for the independent rights of the emperor.*

Book 3

Chapter 1. . . . The present question, then, concerning which we are to make inquiry, lies between two great lights, to wit the Roman pontiff and the Roman prince; and we are to ask whether the authority of the Roman monarch, who is monarch of the world by right, . . . is immediately dependent upon God; or rather on some vicar or minister of God, by whom I understand the successor of Peter, who in very truth bears the keys of the kingdom of heaven. . . .

Chapter 7. They [the defenders of papal supremacy] also allege the oblation of the Magi, from the text of Matthew, saying that Christ received both frankincense and gold to signify that he was lord and ruler of both temporal and spiritual things; whence they infer that the vicar of Christ is lord and ruler of the same, and therefore has authority over both.

In answer to this I admit the text and sense of Matthew, but what they attempt to infer therefrom is faulty in the term. For they syllogize thus: "God is lord of spiritual and temporal things. The supreme pontiff is the vicar of God. Therefore he is lord of spiritual and temporal things." Now both the propositions are true, but the middle is changed and the argument has four terms, which violates the syllogistic form. . . . For God, who is subject of the major premise, is one, and the vicar of God, who is the predicate in the minor, is another.

And should any one insist on the equivalence of vicar the insistence is futile, for no vicariate, divine or human, can be equivalent to the primal authority, as is easily seen. For we know that at any rate with respect to the workings of nature the successor of Peter is not equipotential with the divine authority; for he could not make earth go up or fire come down, in virtue of the office committed to him. . . .

Chapter 13. . . . Now that the authority of the church is not the cause of the imperial authority is thus proved. If, while one thing does not exist or is not exercising its virtue, another thing has its full virtue, the first thing is not the cause of that virtue. But when the church did not exist, or was not exercising its virtue, the empire had its full virtue. Therefore the church is not the cause of the virtue of the empire, and not of its authority either, since its virtue and authority are the same. . . . Paul in the Acts of the Apostles says to Festus, "I stand at the judgment seat of Caesar where I must be judged." . . . And below Paul says again to the Jews in Italy, "Now when the Jews opposed I was compelled to appeal to Caesar, not as having aught of which to accuse my nation, but that I might snatch my soul from death." But if Caesar had not already possessed authority to judge temporal things . . . he who said, "I desire to be released and to be with Christ" [would not] have appealed to a judge who was not competent. . . .

Chapter 16. . . . If man, then, is a kind of mean between corruptible and incorruptible things, since every mean savors of the nature of the extremes, it is necessary that man should savor of either nature. And since every nature is ordained to a certain end it follows that there must be a twofold end of man, so that like as he alone amongst all beings partakes of corruptibility and incorruptibility, so he alone amongst all beings should be ordained for two final goals, of which the one should be his goal as a corruptible being, and the other as an incorruptible.

That unutterable providence, then, has set two ends before man to be contemplated by him; the blessedness, to wit, of this life, which consists in the exercise of his proper power and is figured by the terrestrial paradise, and the blessedness of eternal life, which consists in the fruition of the divine aspect, to which his proper power may not ascend unless assisted by the divine light. And this blessedness is given to be understood by the celestial paradise.

Now to these two as to diverse ends it behooves him to come by diverse means. For to the first we attain by the teachings of philosophy, following them by acting in accordance with the moral and intellectual virtues. To the second by spiritual teachings which transcend human reason, as we follow them by acting according to the theological virtues; faith, hope, to wit, and charity. . . .

Wherefore man had need of a twofold directive power according to his twofold end, to wit, the supreme pontiff to lead the human race, in accordance with things revealed, to eternal life; and the emperor, to direct the human race to temporal felicity in accordance with the teachings of philosophy. And since none, or few (and they with extremest difficulty) could reach this port, were not the waves of seductive greed assuaged and the human race left free to rest in the tranquillity of peace, this is that mark on which he who has charge of the world and is called the Roman prince should chiefly fix his mind, to wit, that on this threshing floor of mortality life should be lived in freedom and in peace. . . .

Thus, then, it is plain that the authority of the temporal monarch descends upon him without any mean from the fountain of universal authority. Which fountain, one in the citadel of its simplicity, flows into manifold channels out of the abundance of its excellence.

From *A Translation of the Latin Works of Dante Alighieri,* by Philip H. Wicksteed. (London: J. M. Dent & Sons Ltd., 1934), pages 226, 246–247, 268–269, 276–279. Used by permission of the publisher.

CHAPTER 8

The Late Middle Ages

In the fourteenth century Europe suffered a series of wars, a devastating plague, and a schism that divided the church between two popes for more than a generation. Theologically, it was a time for asking hard questions—theoretical questions about the path to salvation, practical questions about the corruption of the church.

In philosophy the increasingly dominant nominalist school taught, in its extreme form, that "universal terms" such as "table," "chair," or "human being" have no real existence independent of thought but are merely names *(nomina)* we give to collections of individual objects. Nominalism could undercut the philosophical assumptions behind traditional ways of explaining the Mass or the salvation of "humanity," and the nominalists tended to emphasize the absolute freedom of God's will in a way that undercut efforts to understand reasonable rules God necessarily follows.

Nominalism emphasized the individual in one way, late medieval mysticism did so in another. Most mystics were of course devout and intended to be orthodox, but their claim to a direct experience of God could seem to render the mechanisms of the institutional church redundant. Yet another round in the ongoing debate about Augustine's views on grace potentially had the same effect: while many late medieval theologians insisted on the importance of human efforts toward salvation, those who defended a radically Augustinian view of unmerited grace and therefore of predestination raised doubts about the need for the church's system of discipline and penance.

But widespread criticism of that system arose above all because of its corruption. It came under particularly forceful attack from writers like the Englishman John Wycliffe in the fourteenth century and the Bohemian John Hus at the beginning of the fifteenth. The Great Schism that divided the church between two popes from 1378 to 1415 forced even rather conservative churchmen to question the structure of the church and in particular the absolute authority of the pope. In a situation where no one could agree who was the pope, the "conciliarists" looked to a General Council that might solve the crisis with an authority greater than that of the pope himself.

In the fifteenth century, the Renaissance brought a new humanistic scholarship that valued careful reading of ancient texts, criticized superstition, and suspected that basic Christian ethics might be more important than the increasingly technical theological disputes of the time. Those suspicions, the ongoing theological debates, and the crisis of corruption contributed to the shape of a church ready for radical change, the kind of change that came in the era of the Reformation.

William of Ockham (1285–1347)

From *Philosophical Writings*

Ockham, an English Franciscan, was the greatest of the nominalists, though his own nominalism was carefully qualified—some historians even put him in a separate classification. He did important work in logic and theology and, caught in the middle of a Franciscan battle with Pope John XXII, spent the last years of his life at the imperial court writing anti-papal polemics. These excerpts deal with three points important in Ockham's thought. First, in dealing with the technical question of whether we can have intuitive knowledge of a nonexistent object, Ockham characteristically appeals to the absolute power of God. Second, he defines his own view of universals. Third, he denies the possibility of proving by human reason that there is only one God. These selections obviously include very technical philosophical arguments, but one of their purposes is to emphasize the limits of reason in theology.

2. Whether intuitive cognition can be had of an object that does not exist?

It cannot: For it is a contradiction that there should be an act of seeing and nothing be seen; therefore it is a contradiction that there should be an act of seeing but the seen object not exist.

On the contrary: Vision is a non-relative quality distinct from the object; without contradiction, therefore, it can occur without an object.

On this question I lay down two conclusions. First: Intuitive cognition of a non-existent object is possible by the divine power. I prove this first by the article of faith "I believe in God the Father almighty," which I understand in the following sense: Anything is to be attributed to the divine power, when it does not contain a manifest contradiction. But that this [i.e. cognition of a non-existent object] should be produced by the power of God, does not contain a contradiction; therefore, etc.

Again, on this article is based the famous maxim of the theologians: "Whatever God can produce by means of secondary causes, He can directly produce and preserve without them." From this maxim I argue thus. Every effect which God can produce by means of a secondary cause He can produce directly on His account. God can produce intuitive sense cognition by means of an object; hence He can produce it directly on His own account. . . .

5. . . . That a universal is not a substance existing outside the mind can in the first place be evidently proved as follows: No universal is a substance that is single and numerically one. For if that were supposed, it would follow that Socrates is a universal, since there is no stronger reason for one singular substance to be a universal than for another; therefore no singular substance is a universal, but every substance is numerically one and singular. . . .

Furthermore, if a universal were one substance existing in singular things and distinct from them, it would follow that it could exist apart from them; for every thing naturally prior to another thing can exist apart from it by the power of God. But this consequence is absurd.

Furthermore, if that opinion were true, no individual could be created, but something of the individual would pre-exist; for it would not get its entire being from nothing, if the universal in it has existed before in another individual. For the same reason it would follow that God could not annihilate one individual of a substance, if He did not destroy the other individuals. For if He annihilated one individual, He would destroy the whole of the essence of the individual, and consequently he would destroy that universal which is in it and in others; consequently, the other individuals do not remain, since they cannot remain without a part of themselves, such as the universal is held to be. . . .

Furthermore, it follows that something of the essence of Christ would be miserable and damned; since that common nature which really exists in Christ, really exists in Judas also and is damned.

Therefore, something is both in Christ and in one who is damned, namely in Judas. That, however, is absurd. . . .

From these and many other texts it is clear that a universal is a mental content of such nature as to be predicated of many things. This can also be confirmed by reason. All agree that every universal is predicable of things. But only a mental content or conventional sign, not a substance, is of such nature as to be predicated. Consequently, only a mental content or a conventional sign is a universal. . . .

6. *Can it be proved by natural reason that there is only one God?*

As regards this question, I shall first explain what is meant by the name "God"; secondly I shall answer the question.

Concerning the first point I say that the name "God" can have various descriptions. One of them is: "God is some thing more noble and more perfect than anything else besides Him." Another is: "God is that than which nothing is more noble and more perfect."

Concerning the second point, I maintain that if we understand "God" according to the first description, then it cannot be demonstratively proved that there is only one God. The reason for this is that it cannot be evidently known that God, understood in this sense, exists. Therefore it cannot be evidently known that there is only one God. The inference is plain. The antecedent is proved in this way. The proposition "God exists" is not known by itself, since many doubt it; nor can it be proved from propositions known by themselves, since in every argument something doubtful or derived from faith will be assumed; nor is it known by experience, as is manifest.

Secondly I maintain: If it could be evidently proved that God exists—"God" being understood in the present sense—then the unicity of God could be evidently proved. The reason for this is the following: If there were two Gods, let us call them A and B, then in virtue of our description God A would be more perfect than anything else, therefore God A would be more perfect than God B, and God B would be more imperfect than God A. But God B would also be more perfect than God A, because according to our assumption God B would be God. Consequently God B would be more perfect and more imperfect than God A, and God A than God B, which is a manifest contradiction. If, therefore, it could be evidently proved that God exists—"God" being understood in the present sense—then the unicity of God could be evidently proved.

Thirdly I maintain that the unicity of God cannot be evidently proved if we understand "God" according to the second description.

Yet this negative proposition, "The unicity of God cannot be evidently proved," cannot be proved demonstratively either. For it cannot be demonstrated that the unicity of God cannot be evidently proved, except by rebutting the arguments to the contrary. For instance, it cannot be demonstratively proved that the stars make up an even number, nor can the Trinity of Persons be demonstrated. Nevertheless, these negative propositions, "It cannot be demonstrated that the stars make up an even number," "The Trinity of Persons cannot be demonstrated," cannot be evidently proved.

We must understand, however, that it can be proved that God exists, if we understand "God" according to the second description. For otherwise we could go on *ad infinitum,* if there were not some one among beings to which nothing is prior or superior in perfection. But from this it does not follow that it can be demonstrated that there is only one such being. This we hold only by faith.

Meister Eckhart (c.1260–1327)

From *Sermons*

Eckhart, a German Dominican, was both a popular preacher and a most sophisticated theorist of mysticism. His daring claims for the unity of the ground of the soul with God in mystic experience got him into trouble with the church, and he died while being investigated for heresy.

1

. . . Whatever the soul does, it does through agents. It understands by means of intelligence. If it remembers, it does so by means of memory. If it is to love, the will must be used and thus it acts always through agents and not within its own essence. Its results are achieved through an intermediary. The power of sight can be effectuated only through the eyes, for otherwise the soul has no means of vision. It is the same with the other senses. They are effectuated through intermediaries.

In Being, however, there is no action and, therefore, there is none in the soul's essence. The soul's agents, by which it acts, are derived from the core of the soul. In that core is the central silence, the pure peace, and abode of the heavenly birth, the place for this event: this utterance of God's word. By nature the core of the soul is sensitive to nothing but the divine Being, unmediated. Here God enters the soul with all he has and not in part. He enters the soul through its core and nothing may touch that core except God himself. . . .

God has perfect insight into himself and knows himself up and down, through and through, not by ideas, but of himself. God begets his Son through the true unity of the divine nature. See! This is the way: he begets his Son in the core of the soul and is made One with it. There is no other way. If an idea were interposed, there could be no true unity. Man's whole blessedness lies in that unity.

Now you might say: "Naturally! But there is nothing to the soul but ideas." No! Not at all! If that were so, the soul could never be blessed, for even God cannot make a creature in which a perfect blessing is found. Otherwise, God himself would not be the highest blessing, or the best of ends, as it is his nature and will to be—the beginning and the end of everything. A blessing is not a creature nor is it perfection, for perfection [that is, in all virtues] is the consequence of the perfecting of life, and for that you must get into the essence, the core of the soul, so that God's undifferentiated essence may reach you there, without the interposition of any idea. . . .

23

. . . The hearing of God's Word requires complete self-surrender. He who hears and that which is heard are identical constituents of the eternal Word. What the eternal Father teaches is his own Being, Nature, and Godhead—which he is always revealing through his only begotten Son. He teaches that we are to be identical with him.

To deny one's self is to be the only begotten Son of God and one who does so has for himself all the properties of that Son. All God's acts are performed and his teachings conveyed through the Son, to the point that we should be his only begotten Son. And when this is accomplished in God's sight, he is so fond of us and so fervent that he acts as if his divine Being might be shattered and he himself annihilated if the whole foundations of his Godhead were not revealed to us, together with his nature and being. God makes haste to do this, so that it may be ours as it is his. It is here that God finds joy and rapture in fulfillment and the person who is thus within God's knowing and love becomes just what God himself is. . . .

Speaking to this point, St. Paul says: "I could wish to be cut off eternally from God for my friends' sake and for God's sake." To be cut off from God for an instant is to be cut off from him forever, and to be cut off from God at all is the pain of hell. What, then, does St. Paul mean by saying that he could wish to be cut off from God? The authorities question whether or not St. Paul, when he made this remark, was already perfect or only on the road to perfection. I say that he was already quite perfect, for otherwise he would not have said it and now I shall explain why St. Paul says that he could wish to be cut off from God.

Man's last and highest parting occurs when, for God's sake, he takes leave of god. St. Paul took leave of god for God's sake and gave up all that he might get from god, as well as all he might give—together with every idea of god. In parting with these, he parted with god for God's sake and yet God remained to him as God is in his own nature—not as he is conceived by anyone to be—nor yet as something to be achieved—but more as an "is-ness," as God really is. Then he neither gave to God nor received anything from him, for he and God were a unit, that is pure unity. . . .

God gives to all things alike and as they proceed from God they are alike. Angels, men, and creatures all flow out of God in whom their prime origin is. Take them as they first emanate from him and you will find them all alike, but, if they are alike in temporal sphere, in eternity and in God they are the much more so. A flea, to the extent that it is in God, ranks above the highest angel in his own right. Thus, in God, all things are equal and are God himself.

In this likeness or identity God takes such delight that he pours his whole nature and being into it. His pleasure is as great, to take a simile, as that of a horse, let loose to run over a green heath where the ground is level and smooth, to gallop as a horse will, as fast as he can over greensward—for this is a horse's pleasure and expresses his nature. It is so with God. It is his pleasure and rapture to discover identity, because he can always put his whole nature into it—for he is this identity itself.

From *Meister Eckhart: A Modern Translation,* translated by Raymond B. Blakney, pages 95–99, 203–205. Copyright, 1941, by Harper & Brothers. Reprinted by permission of Harper & Row, Publishers, Inc.

Julian of Norwich (1342–c.1420)

From *Revelations of Divine Love*

Julian, an Englishwoman of limited education, experienced a series of visions, the first at a moment of near-mortal illness. Her reflections on her experience form a classic document of mysticism—not least because of her always present common sense. Some of these selections illustrate her particularly interesting use of feminine imagery for God.

Chapter 2. These revelations were shewed to a simple unlearned creature living in this mortal flesh, in the year of our Lord one thousand three hundred and seventy-three, on the thirteenth day of May. . . .

Chapter 3. And when I was thirty years and a half, God sent me a bodily sickness; in which I lay three days and three nights. And on the fourth night I received all the rites of the Holy Church, and thought not to have lived till day. And after this I lay two days and two nights more. And on the third night, I thought oftentimes that I would pass away; and so thought they that were with me. And yet in this time I felt a great loathsomeness to die—not for anything of earth that I wished to live for, nor for any pain that I was afraid of (for I trusted in God and his mercy), but for this: I wished to live in order to love God better and for a longer time, that I might, by the grace of that living, have more knowing and loving of God in the bliss of heaven. . . .

My curate was sent for to be present at my end. Before he came, my eyes were fixed upwards, and I could not speak. He set the cross before my face, and said: "I have brought the image of thy Saviour; look thereupon, and comfort thee therewith." But I believe I was well enough; for my eyes were set upwards into heaven whither I trusted to come by the mercy of God. Nevertheless, I consented to turn my eyes to confront the crucifix, if I could. And so I did. . . .

Chapter 4. And in this time, suddenly I saw the red blood running down from under the garland, hot and fresh, plenteous and life-like, just as it was in the time that the garland of thorns was pressed down on his blessed head. Even so I conceived truly that it was himself, God and man, the same that suffered for me, who shewed it to me—without any intermediary.

In the same shewing, suddenly the Trinity filled full my heart with the utmost joy (thus I understood it shall be in heaven without end unto all that come thither). For the Trinity is God and God is the Trinity. The Trinity is our Maker. The Trinity is our Keeper. The Trinity is our everlasting lover. The Trinity is our endless Joy and our Bliss, by our Lord Jesus Christ and in our Lord Jesus Christ. And this was shewed in the first sight and in them all. For where Jesus appeareth, the Blessed Trinity is understood, as I see it. . . .

Chapter 58. God the blissful Trinity—which is everlasting Being, right as he is endless from without-beginning, right so it was in his endless purpose to make man's kind. . . .

And thus, in our making, God almighty is our kindly Father: and God all-wisdom is our kindly Mother: with the love and goodness of the Holy Ghost; which is all one God, one Lord. And in the knitting and the oneing he is our very true Spouse, and we his loved wife and his fair maiden. With which wife he was never displeased; for he saith: "I love thee, and thou lovest me, and our love shall never be parted in two."

I beheld the working of all the blessed Trinity. In which beholding I saw and understood these three properties: the property of the Fatherhood, and the property of the Motherhood, and the property of the Lordship—in one God. In our Father almighty we have our keeping and our bliss, in respect of our kindly substance (which is applied to us by our creation), from without-beginning. And in the second Person, in understanding and wisdom, we have our keeping in respect of our sensuality, our restoring and our saving. (For he is our Mother, Brother and Saviour.) And in our good Lord the Holy Ghost we have our rewarding and our enrichment for our living and our travail: which, of his high plenteous grace, and in his marvellous courtesy, endlessly surpasseth all that we desire.

For all our life is in three. In the first we have our being: and in the second we have our increasing: and in the third we have our fulfilling. The first is kind: the second is mercy: the third is grace. For the first: I saw and understood that the high might of the Trinity is our Father, and the deep wisdom of the Trinity is our Mother, and the great love of the Trinity is our Lord. And all these we have in kind and in our substantial making.

And furthermore, I saw that the second Person, who is our Mother substantially—the same very dear Person is now become our

Mother sensually. For of God's making we are double: that is to say, substantial and sensual. Our substance is that higher part which we have in our Father, God almighty. And in the second Person of the Trinity is our Mother in kind, in our substantial making—in whom we are grounded and rooted; and he is our Mother of mercy, in taking our sensuality. And thus "our Mother" meaneth for us different manners of his working, in whom our parts are kept unseparated. For in our Mother Christ, we have profit and increase; and in mercy he re-formeth and restoreth us: and by the power of his passion, his death and his uprising, oned us to our substance. Thus worketh our Mother in mercy to all his beloved children who are docile and obedient to him. . . .

Chapter 59. . . . And thus is Jesus our true Mother in kind, of our first making; and he is our true Mother in grace by his taking of our made kind. All the fair working and all the sweet kindly offices of our most dear Motherhood are appropriated to the second Person. For in him we have this godly will whole and secure without end, both in kind and in grace, of his own proper goodness. I understand three types of beholding of Motherhood in God. The first is the ground of making of our kind. The second is the taking of our kind—and there beginneth the Motherhood of grace. The third is Motherhood in working. And therein is a forth-spreading, by the same grace, of a length and breadth, of a height and deepness without end. And all is one love.

From *The Revelations of Divine Love of Julian of Norwich,* pages 47, 49–51, 158–160, 162, translated by James Walsh. Harper & Brothers, 1961. © James Walsh, S.J., 1961. Used by permission of Burns & Oates.

Robert Holcot (d. 1349)

From *Lectures on the Wisdom of Solomon*

Holcot, an English Dominican, was influenced by Ockham's philosophy. Desiring to preserve God's absolute freedom, he nevertheless sought a way to guarantee the normal operation of the usual means of grace. Like many nominalist theologians, he therefore distinguished between the absolute power of God in principle and rules to which God in practice submits himself.

Chapter 3, Lecture 35

Question: Can man assisted by grace earn eternal life by his own full merit *(ex condigno)*? . . .

Solution: Now as to the original question, we can answer that the statement, man assisted by grace can earn eternal life by his own full merit, can be understood in two ways. It can be understood according to the natural value of man's action or according to its contracted value. Man would earn salvation according to natural value if his merit were, by its very nature and existence, such that eternal life would be suitable payment for it. According to contracted value, the value of one's merit would be determined by legal arrangement in the way that a small copper coin which, in natural value, has not the same weight or worth as a loaf of bread is assigned this value by the law of the land.

Now if we understand man's merit according to the first interpretation, the natural goodness of our works does not earn eternal life fully *(de condigno)* but only partially *(de congruo)*, since it is appropriate *(congruens)* that if man has done all that he can with his finite resources God should reward him with His infinite resources.

But according to the second understanding of merit we can say that our works are fully worthy of eternal life, not because of any merit inherent in the acts themselves but because of grace, since our Lord has established that he who does good works in a state of grace shall receive eternal life. Therefore, through the law and grace of our ruler Christ we merit eternal life by our own full merit *(de condigno)*. . . .

Chapter 12, Lecture 145

Question: Is God required to give grace to the man who prepares himself for its reception? . . .

Solution: To those who doubt such an affirmation, it may be said that there is a distinction between compulsory necessity and unfailing necessity [that is, consistency]. With God compulsory necessity has no place, but an unfailing necessity is appropriate to God because of His promise, that is, His Covenant, or established law. This is not an absolute but rather a conditional necessity. According to God's established law the pilgrim who does whatever he can to dispose himself for grace always receives grace. However, if He should choose to, God could deviate from His law for someone other than the pilgrim or the devil. Then, however much such a person [with whom God has not made His Covenant] might dispose himself for grace, he would not receive it. Man's disposition does not require the giving of grace except by congruency, because grace surpasses every natural act; it is impossible for man to fully merit *(de condigno)* through any natural act.

Translated by Paul L. Nyhus. From Heiko A. Oberman, *Forerunners of the Reformation* (New York: Holt, Rinehart & Winston, 1966; Philadelphia: Fortress Press, 1981), pages 142–143, 148–149. Copyright © 1966 by Heiko A. Obermann. Used by permission of Holt, Rinehart & Winston.

Thomas Bradwardine (1290–1349)

From *The Cause of God Against the Pelagians*

To a radical Augustinian like Bradwardine, even the qualified talk of rewarding human merit he encountered in such contemporaries as Holcot seemed Pelagian, and he wrote this treatise to denounce "the pestilential Pelagians." Bradwardine taught at Oxford and eventually became Archbishop of Canterbury shortly before he died of the Black Death.

The Pelagians now oppose our whole presentation of predestination and reprobation, attempting either to eliminate them completely or, at least, to show that they are dependent on personal merits. . . .

(3) The Gospel of John states: "He gave them power to become sons of God." Since, therefore, in accordance with predestination and grace men become sons of God, this lies within their own free power and occurs in no other way than by merits acceptable to God. . . .

(7) Likewise, since it would be unfair and cruel for either man or angel to harm someone without provocation, and such an action would be necessarily unjust, how much less befitting would such action be for a God who is the most right and the most righteous? Nor would it befit God that anyone should be reprobated and predestined to eternal fire unless it were done on account of preceding guilt. . . .

(3) Now when they bring forward the quotation from the Gospel of John, "He gave them power to become sons of God," they seem

to wish to conclude from this that some become or can become the elect sons of God in the course of their life. That is, that from the number of those who are not predestined or who are reprobate, some at the present time can become predestined and at the same time cease to belong to the reprobate. . . .

The quotation from the Gospel of John seems rather to prove the opposite. For he did not say, "He gave them power to make themselves sons of God," but "to be made sons of God." But by whom? Not by themselves. Not out of their own will. Whoever has produced himself? Whoever was born out of himself? What son of the devil can give birth to himself and appear to be the son of God? Hear what follows: ". . . who are born not from human flesh or will but from God." Therefore they do not make themselves sons of God. God does this. . . .

God gives men power, that is to say, a rational soul and free will with which man can freely and voluntarily receive grace in the present and glory in the future so that, in both the present and the future, they might become sons of God. Thus in the present, as they are being made sons of God by faith and prevenient grace, which makes them into adopted sons of God, they freely accomplish the pleasing work of sons and so freely persevere in this to such an extent that no one could take away their sonship unless they would permit it. . . .

We cannot walk in faith without being in grace. How would we ever have received this grace? By our preceding merits? Grace is *given* to you, it is not a payment. For this reason it is called grace, because it is freely given. With preceding merits you cannot buy what you have already received as a gift. Therefore the sinner has received first grace in order that his sins might be forgiven. What has he merited? When he demands justice he will receive punishment and when he asks for mercy he will receive grace. But this is exactly what had been promised by God through the prophets. . . .

(7) Now we turn to the argument which accuses God of injustice and cruelty. . . .

Peter Lombard* shows that there are five reasons for man's punishment in this dispensation, which are: (1) the correction of sin, (2) the beginning of punishment for sin, (3) the growth in merits, as it was in the cases of Job and Tobith, (4) the avoidance of sin, as

---

* Peter Lombard (c.1095–1160) was the author of the most widely used textbook in medieval theology.

Paul says about the thorn in his flesh, (5) the glory of God, as John makes clear in his passage about the man blind from birth [John 9:3]. One can also be publicly punished, to frighten others, to deter them from evil and strengthen them in goodness, in accordance with the laws, be they divine, canonical, or civil. If a man may undergo temporal punishment for the temporal benefit of others, why should he not be punished temporally and eternally for the temporal and eternal benefit of the elect, in order that they might all the more flee from evil and choose the good in the present, that in the future they might have greater joy, deeper love, and higher praise for God?

Thus great profit, both in the present and in the future, accrues to the elect from the reprobate, indeed the whole purpose of being for the reprobate is that they have been created for the sake of the elect. What injustice and cruelty can be charged to God because He chooses to predestine and create one of His creatures for the service of another creature and both of them for His own service, praise, glory, and honor? This is particularly true, since He punishes no man with eternal damnation unless such a man deserves it, that is to say, unless through his sins he deservedly and justly requires eternal punishment. And God always punishes most mercifully and appropriately because innumerable times he finds a way to punish less than is deserved. . . .

Why do they not accuse God because He punishes innocent beasts and baptized infants with no small physical pain? Indeed He gave up his own most innocent Son, our Lord Jesus Christ, to a most painful, cruel, and tormenting punishment. But since God is omnipotent, completely free Lord of His whole creation, whose will alone is the most righteous law for all creation—if He should eternally punish the innocent, particularly since He does it for the perfection of the universe, for the profit of others, and for the honor of God Himself, who would presume to dispute with Him, to contradict Him, or ask, "Why do you do this?" I firmly believe, no one! "Has the potter no right over the clay to make of the same lump one vessel for honor and another for menial use?" [Rom. 9:21].

Translated by Paul L. Nyhus. From Heiko A. Oberman, *Forerunners of the Reformation* (New York: Holt, Rinehart & Winston, 1966; Philadelphia: Fortress Press, 1981), pages 151–152, 154, 156, 161–162. Copyright © 1966 by Heiko A. Obermann. Used by permission of Holt, Rinehart & Winston.

John Wycliffe (c.1330–1384)

From *On the Pastoral Office*

Wycliffe studied and taught at Oxford and soon became involved in English efforts to clean up corruption in the church, winning the patronage of the English nobleman John of Gaunt, who wanted an excuse to exercise his own power over church officials. In the end Wycliffe was condemned as a heretic, but English Reformers later identified him as one of their precursors—perhaps above all because he began the task of translating the Bible into English. In his day the official position of the English church was that those without enough education to read Latin should study the Bible only by listening to preachers, where they could be guided by those trained in such matters. Wycliffe took a different view.

1. . . . Now there are two things which pertain to the status of pastor: the holiness of the pastor and the wholesomeness of his teaching. He ought to be holy, so strong in every sort of virtue that he would rather desert every kind of human intercourse, all the temporal things of this world, even mortal life itself, before he would sinfully depart from the truth of Christ. . . .

2. From this principle of faith, which can signally be called by the faithful "golden," plainly is derived the rule which the apostle has handed down, "Having food and wherewith we are clothed let us be content." This is clear: each one ought, to the limit of his ability, to follow Christ in his manner of life. But each priest, curate, or pastor has the ability so to follow Christ in his manner of life; therefore he should do it. This moved the apostles and the other priests of the Lord after them to imitate Christ in this evangelical poverty. . . .

4. . . . But now our prelates are perverted on the side of the devil, not so sustaining the poor by hospitality, but rather secular lords and tyrants, who do not need such alms, but are commonly gorged with inhuman and gluttonous feasts, and yet are satiated sumptuously without a qualm from the goods of the poor. . . .

5. On this basis one assumes that all curates ought according to the law of the Lord to be induced to live solely upon the material alms of their subjects. For if they possess sufficient revenues or worldly wealth, they ought to relinquish them in favor of the material alms of their flock. When food is elsewhere lacking, they ought

in recompense of charity to live from such alms of their subjects, and thus to distribute more worthy alms (because they are spiritual). . . .

6. From these principles one concludes that a curate ought not to extort tithes from his subjects through excommunication or other censures, and it is clear therefore that a curate ought not to quarrel with his subjects concerning such matters. Christ and his apostles indicated this by not so exacting tithes, being satisfied instead with needful food and clothing. . . .

7. From this the faithful infer that a curate ought not through censures or other temporal threats to give to his lord prelate tribute from the alms of the people subject to him, which cannot be established from the law of the Lord. For if pope, cardinal, bishop, or archdeacon require such tribute from a subject curate, it is certain that such requisition is unjust, for it is not founded in the law of the Lord; and the whole business ends in the spoliation of the poor subjects. . . .

Part II

2. "Among all the duties of the pastor after justice of life, holy preaching is most to be praised," for Christ, the Primal Truth, . . . said to the woman commending the one who bore him in the womb and nourished his body, "They are blessed who hear the word of God and keep it." . . . It is evident that preaching the gospel is the special work of the curate, for Christ advances more in his apostles by preaching to the people than by doing any miracle which in his own person he did in Judea. . . . Preaching the gospel exceeds prayer and administration of the sacraments, to an infinite degree. . . . Spreading the gospel has far wider and more evident benefit; it is thus the most precious activity of the Church. . . .

2a. The friars with their followers say that it is heresy thus to write God's law in English and make it known to ignorant men. . . .

It seems first that the knowledge of God's law should be taught in that language which is best known, because this knowledge is God's Word. When Christ says in the Gospel that both heaven and earth shall pass away but his words shall not pass away, he means by his "words" his knowledge. Thus God's knowledge is Holy Scripture that may in no wise be false. Also the Holy Spirit gave to the apostles at Pentecost knowledge to know all manner of languages to teach the people God's law thereby; and so God willed that the people be taught his laws in divers tongues. But what man on God's behalf should reverse God's ordinance and his will? For this reason Saint Jerome labored and translated the Bible from divers tongues into Latin that it might after be translated into other tongues. Thus Christ and his apostles taught the people in that tongue that was best known to them. Why should men not do so now?

Translated by Ford Lewis Battles. From *Advocates of Reform,* edited by Matthew Spinka (Volume XIV: The Library of Christian Classics), pages 32–33, 35–37, 48–50. First published in MCMLIII by the SCM Press Ltd., London, and The Westminster Press, Philadelphia. Used by permission of the publishers.

Dietrich of Niem (c.1340–1418)

From *Ways of Uniting and Reforming the Church*

Dietrich represents conciliarism in radical form. Faced with two men—and eventually three—with a claim to be pope, some theologians developed qualified accounts of how a council might settle the matter in such an emergency, without challenging papal supremacy under normal conditions. Dietrich, on the other hand, set out a full account of the superiority of councils to popes as a matter of principle.

Disciple: . . . The Church of Christ, duly ordained by him, is superior, more honorable, and more worthy of respect than all [other] societies and organizations. This is obvious. These others are the temporal assemblies of the people, but she is the spiritual congregation of the people. These exist for a time, but she even to the end shall never fail. These save the body that perishes, but she the soul that endures forever. . . .

Master: But tell me, I pray, what Church do you mean? St. Athanasius in the Creed spoke of "the one, holy, Catholic, and the Apostolic Church." For if the Catholic [Church] and the Apostolic Church are the same, then it was superfluous to repeat what could have been explained by one word. If, however, they are not the same, wherein do they differ?

Disciple: Indeed, as you well know, the Universal Church is made up of various members of Greeks, Latins, and barbarians who believe in Christ, of men and women, of peasants and nobles, of poor and rich, constituting one body, which is called Catholic. The head of this body, the Universal Church, is Christ alone. The others such as the pope, the cardinals and prelates, the clerics, the kings and princes, and the common people, are the members, occupying their various positions. The pope cannot and ought not to be called the head of this Church, but only the vicar of Christ, his viceregent on earth, yet only while the key does not err. In this Church and in its faith every man can be saved, even if in the whole world a pope cannot be found, the reason being that upon this Church alone has the faith of Christ been grounded, and to this Church alone has the power of binding and loosing been handed down. For suppose there were no pope, but only one faithful person: even then the power of binding and loosing would be available. In this Church are the seven sacraments and our entire salvation. This Church has never been able to err, according to the current law, never been able to fail, has never suffered schism, has never been stained by heresy, has never been able to be deceived or to deceive, and has never sinned. . . . For in this Church all the faithful, in so far as they are faithful, are one in Christ, in whose faith there is no differentiation between Jew and Greek, master and slave.

The other is called the Apostolic particular and private Church. It is included in the Catholic Church, and is made up of the pope, the cardinals, the bishops, the prelates, and the churchmen. It is usually called the Roman Church, whose head is believed to be the pope; the others are, however, included in it as superior and inferior members. This Church may err, and may have erred, may deceive and be deceived, may suffer schism and heresy and may even fail [*deficere*]. This Church is seen to be of far less authority than the Universal Church, as will be pointed out below. It embodies the instrumental and operative functions of the keys of the Universal Church and exercises its power of binding and loosing. It does not have and, in good conscience, cannot have greater authority or power than that which is granted to it by the Universal Church. These two Churches, therefore, differ as genus and species, since all of the Apostolic Church is Catholic, but not the other way around. . . .

Master: Which Church, then, must we labor to restore and unite?

Disciple: Indeed, laying aside all else, we must labor for the well-being of this Universal Church and for the sake of those of the faithful who have erred and gone astray by reuniting that second Church, the Apostolic, since apart from the Universal Church there is no salvation.

Master: Who will first undertake to lead back the erring members and procure a union?

Disciple: Actually, when the pope is not suspected, and when there is no question over the union of the head, this [task] belongs in the first place to him. At other times it belongs, I believe, to the whole congregation of bishops, prelates, and secular princes, or their greater part. Whatever they shall have done in this situation is to be accepted as if it were a matter of faith.

Master: What have seculars to do with the restoration of the Church and the uniting of its members?

Disciple: Surely if you love the truth and peace, if you have any regard for the common good, if you consider the natural body, how the hand comes to the help of the whole body, and each limb hastens to its defense, then we ought also to attend to the uniting, pacifying, and restoring of the Church. . . . Not merely the secular princes but the peasants, the husbandmen, indeed every one in so far as he is able, even the least of the faithful, ought to come to her help, and must, if necessary, risk death for the well-being of the whole flock. . . .

Master: But why should we labor for the union of the Universal Church, if that Church is, and always has been, undivided, one, and has never suffered schism?

Disciple: My Father, if it please you to attend, I do not say that the Universal Church can be reunited since she cannot be divided by schism, because she can even be preserved in one individual; but I say that we must labor for her unity, that is, for the harmony and pacification of her members. . . .

Today the unity of the head is lost, for three dare to call themselves pope. Today there is a division among the members, for obedience and submission is granted to every one of them. Today there is a disappearance, nay, a complete abandonment, of good moral practices, for simony, avarice, the sale of benefices, tyranny, and cruelty hold sway, approved as it were by wont amongst the ecclesiastics. . . .

Here let us consider the pope. He is a man of the earth, clay from clay, a sinner liable to sin, but two days ago the son of a poor peasant. It is he who has been created pope. Has he without any penance for his sins, without confession, without contrition become an angel, unable to sin? Has he become a saint? Who made him a saint? Not the Holy Spirit, because the office is not wont to bestow the Holy Spirit but the grace and love of God alone; and not the authority, which is communicated to both the good and the evil. Therefore the pope cannot become an angel. A pope as pope is a man and as pope can sin even as a man can err. . . .

Again, the pope is not above the gospel of God. For if he were, his authority would be greater than the authority of Christ, and then his power would not be derived from Christ. But he is subject in all things to the precept and command of Christ as is any other Christian. . . .

Elsewhere I have said that, when the reformation of the Universal Church and the case of the pope is discussed . . . the summoning of a general council in no way belongs to the pope, even though he be the sole universal and undoubted pope. It does not even belong to him to preside as judge or to define anything having to do with the state of the Church. This [prerogative] belongs primarily to the bishops, cardinals, patriarchs, secular princes, communities, and the rest of the faithful. A man of ill report cannot and must not, from the point of view of what is right, be a judge, particularly in his own case, when, for the sake of the common welfare, the resignation and deprivation of a private individual's advantage and honor is the aim. Therefore, according to the example of the ancients, the bishops, the secular princes, the communities, and the ecclesiastics will summon [a council to meet] in some suitable, safe place, having the necessities of life in abundance, and will also summon to this [council] those contending for the papacy. . . .

Out of the number [of prelates, cardinals, bishops, and temporal lords] some will be selected who could and ought to preside in this general council. . . .

Master: Is not such a council in which the pope does not preside above the pope?

Disciple: Certainly. It is superior in authority, dignity, and function. The pope himself is bound to obey such a council in all things. Such a council can limit the power of the pope. To such a council, as it represents the Church Universal, the keys of binding and loosing were granted. Such a council can take away the papal rights. From such a council no one can appeal. Such a council can set up new laws, and destroy old ones. The constitutions, statutes, and regulations of such a council are immutable and cannot be set aside by any person inferior to the council.

Translated by James Kerr Cameron. From *Advocates of Reform,* edited by Matthew Spinka (Volume XIV: The Library of Christian Classics), pages 150–153, 155, 159–160. First published in MCMLIII by the SCM Press Ltd., London, and The Westminster Press, Philadelphia. Used by permission of the publishers.

John Hus (1372–1415)

From *On Simony*

*Hus led a popular movement in Bohemia, attacking church corrup-
tion and favoring greater popular participation in church affairs. The
Council of Constance vindicated conciliarism and ended the schism
by replacing the three extant popes with its own choice, but it then set
limits on its sympathy for reform by condemning and burning Hus.
His followers continued as a popular movement in Bohemia, and
Luther saw Hus as an important precursor. This selection shows the
forcefulness of his attacks on church corruption.*

Simony, as the word signifies, is trafficking in holy things. And
since both he who buys and he who sells is a merchant, a simoniac
is both he who buys and he who sells holy things. *Consequently,
simony comprises both buying and selling of holy things. . . .*

Whenever anyone confers a spiritual gift improperly either himself
or through another, either openly or covertly, either in consideration
of service, or material gift, or human favor, he thereby commits
simony, contrary to the Scriptures and Christ's command, "Freely
have ye received, freely give." The apostles received freely, without
bribery, without unworthy subservience, or material favor; therefore,
they likewise gave freely, without such bribery. But since now clergy
do not receive freely, they likewise do not give freely, neither absolu-
tion, nor ordination, nor extreme unction, nor other spiritual things.

From this exposition, as well as from the customs which we plainly
observe among clerics, we may learn that there are but few priests
who have secured their ordination or their benefices without simony,
so they on the one hand and their bishops on the other have fallen
into simony. And since simony is heresy, if anyone observe carefully
he must perceive that many are heretics. . . .

They are like their father, Simon the magician who, having been
baptized and having become an adherent of Saint Philip, offered the
apostles money that he might receive power from them. Saint Luke
writes about him: "Now when Simon saw that through the laying on
of the apostles' hands the Holy Spirit was given, he offered them
money, saying, Give me also this power that on whomsoever I lay
my hands, he may receive the Holy Spirit" [Acts 8:18–19]. Therefore, all those who buy or sell the gifts of God, either for money or

for some other consideration, or knowingly aid in such traffic, are called simoniacs, or in Czech *svatokupci*. . . .

From this pious exposition one may understand how perverse are the practices in regard to the appointment of bishops of our day and our times. For formerly the custom prevailed that either our loving Lord appointed the bishop by means of a revelation or the people . . . elected him. But nowadays the power of the people to request or elect a worthy priest is denied them; and a way is thus opened for avaricious or otherwise dishonorable men to buy people from the pope as if they were cattle, for the material profit of the buyers. . . .

But I know three persons who could help in preventing this evil, if the Lord were to manifest his grace in them: The first of them is the pope, if the Lord granted one who would destroy all simony according to the Scriptures and the enactments of holy bishops. But when will such a pope come forth? It would indeed be a great miracle if he should now make his appearance. Moreover, I know that his apostles would not let him remain alive for long!

The second and more likely help would come if secular princes and lords, having been divinely instructed, would forbid the trafficking and the irregular appointments of unworthy prelates over the people. . . .

But immediately there rushes out of the forest a wild boar, digging up Christ's vineyard and uprooting, saying, "The kings, lords, or any other seculars have no right to rule over the spirituals!" I answer, in the first place, that throughout the Old Testament [period] kings ruled the priests and bishops. For King Solomon deposed the highest bishop Abiathar from the priesthood and sent him back to his fields, and appointed Zadok in his place. And he did this in accordance with God's will, as the Scriptures testify. . . .

Secondly, I say that because every king receives the power over his kingdom from God so that he may rule it in truth and justice, and since priests constitute a part of that kingdom, he should rule over them in truth and justice. He does not rule over them in truth and justice if he allows them to live in plain opposition to the supreme King, but, like a careless servant, he thus proves himself unworthy of his royal office. . . .

If kings, princes, and lords, having been instructed in God's law, were to forbid priests to practice simony and themselves refrain from it, the Lord would grant them peace in their realm, praise, and prosperity, and afterwards the Kingdom of Heaven. O faithful kings, princes, lords, and knights! awake from the fell dream into which the priests have lulled you, and drive out the simoniacal heresy from your territories.

Translated by Matthew Spinka. From *Advocates of Reform,* edited by Matthew Spinka (Volume XIV: The Library of Christian Classics), pages 201, 203, 209, 269, 272–273, 275. First published in MCMLIII by the SCM Press Ltd., London, and The Westminster Press, Philadelphia. Used by permission of the publishers.

Desiderius Erasmus (c.1469–1536)

From *The Praise of Folly*

Erasmus was the greatest of the humanists of northern Europe. He was most famous for his edition of the Greek New Testament, but this selection shows many of his characteristic concerns—a love of scholarship and peace; a suspicion of superstition, conflict, and theological technicalities. It represents an attitude of mind characteristic of the Renaissance but out of place on either the Protestant or the Catholic side after the Reformation began. When that conflict came, Erasmus remained a Catholic, though he tried, unsuccessfully, to speak for moderation. At the beginning of this selection "Folly" is speaking of her allies and friends.

A group that does belong with us beyond any doubt is made up of those who enjoy telling and hearing monstrous lies and tall tales. They never get enough of ghosts and goblins and the like. They are most pleased by stories that are farthest from the truth. Such wonders are a diversion from boredom, and they may also be very profitable, especially for priests and pardoners.

Closely related are those who have reached the foolish but comforting belief that if they gaze on a picture of Polyphemus-Christopher, they will not die that day; or that whoever speaks the right words to an image of Barbara will return unharmed from battle; or that a novena to Erasmus, with proper prayers and candles, will shortly make one rich. In St. George they have turned up another Hercules or Hippolytus. They all but adore his horse, which is piously studded and ornamented, and they ingratiate themselves by small gifts. To swear by St. George's brass helmets is an oath for a king. Then, what shall I say of those who happily delude themselves with forged pardons for their sins? They calculate the time to be spent in Purgatory down to the year, month, day, and hour, as if from a fool-proof mathematical table. There are also those who propose to get everything they desire by relying on magical charms and prayers devised by some pious impostor for the sake of his soul, or for profit. They will have wealth, honor, pleasure, plenty, good health, long life, a vigorous old age, and at last, a place next to Christ in heaven. However, they don't want that seat of honor until the very last minute; celestial pleasures may come only when worldly pleasures, hung on to with tooth and nail, finally depart.

I picture a business man, a soldier, or a judge taking from all his loot one small coin as a proper expiation for the infinite evil of his life. He thinks it possible to buy up, like notes, so many perjuries, rapes, debauches, fights, murders, frauds, lies and treacheries. Having done this, he feels free to start with a clean slate on a new round of sin. . . .

Why should I go farther on this sea of superstition? "If I had a hundred tongues, a hundred mouths, a voice of brass, I could not describe all the forms of folly, or list all its names." The life of Christians everywhere runs over with such nonsense. Superstitions are allowed and even promoted by the priests; they do not regret anything so profitable. Imagine, in the midst of this, some insolent wise men speaking the real truth: "You will not die badly if you live well. Your sins are redeemed if to the payment of money you add tears, vigils, prayers, fastings, and hatred of evil, and if you change your whole way of living. The saints will favor you if you imitate them." A wise man who snarled out things like that would throw the world into turmoil and deprive it of happiness! . . .

Perhaps it would be wise to pass over the theologians in silence. . . . Their opinion of themselves is so great that they behave as if they were already in heaven; they look down pityingly on other men as so many worms. A wall of imposing definitions, conclusions, corollaries, and explicit and implicit propositions protects them. . . . They are full of big words and newly-invented terms.

They explain (to suit themselves) the most difficult mysteries: how the world was created and set in order; through what channels original sin has passed to successive generations; by what means, in what form, and for how long the perfect Christ was in the womb of the Virgin; and how accidents subsist in the Eucharist without their subject. But these are nothing. Here are questions worthy of these great and reputedly illuminated theologians. If they encounter these questions they will have to extend themselves. Was divine generation at a particular instant? Are there several sonships in Christ? Is this a possible proposition: God the Father hates the Son? Could God have assumed the form of a woman, a devil, an ass, a gourd, a stone? If so, how could the gourd have preached, performed miracles, and been crucified? What would Peter have consecrated if he had administered the sacrament when Christ's body hung on the Cross? . . .

There are in addition those moral maxims, or rather contradictions, that make the so-called Stoic paradoxes seem like child's play. For example: it is less of a sin to cut the throats of a thousand men than to stitch a poor man's shoe on Sunday; it is better to commit the whole world to destruction than to tell a single lie, even a white one. These subtlest of subtleties are made more subtle by the methods of the scholastic philosophers. It is easier to escape from a maze than from the tangles of Realists, Nominalists, Thomists, Albertists, Occamists, and Scotists,* to name the chief ones only. There is so much erudition and obscurity in the various schools that I imagine the apostles themselves would need some other spiritual assistance if they were to argue these topics with modern theologians.

Paul could exhibit faith, but when he said, "Faith is the substance of things hoped for, the evidence of things not seen," he did not define it scholastically. Although he exemplified charity supremely well, he analyzed and defined it with little logical subtlety in his first epistle to the Corinthians, Chapter Thirteen. No doubt the apostles consecrated the Eucharist devoutly; but suppose you had examined them about the *terminus a quo* and the *terminus ad quem,* † or about transubstantiation: in what way the body is in many places at once; the difference between the body of Christ in heaven, on the Cross, and in the sacrament; and the point at which transubstantiation takes place, considering the fact that the prayer effecting it is a distinct quantity in time. I rather doubt if they would have answered you as acutely as the Scotists do. . . .

Similarly, the apostles teach grace, and yet they never distinguished between the grace that is freely given and the grace that makes one deserving. They urge good works without defining work, work worked, and work working. They always preach charity; yet

---

* These are all schools of medieval philosophy: for the nominalists, see the introduction to this chapter; the realists were their opponents, who believed in the "real existence" of universals. Erasmus then mentions the followers of Thomas Aquinas, Albert the Great, William of Ockham, and John Duns Scotus.

† Limit from which; limit to which.

they do not separate innate from acquired charity, nor explain whether charity is an accident or a substance, created or uncreated.

Suggestions
for Further Reading

There are thick volumes devoted to the secondary literature on specific periods, topics, and even individual theologians; a brief list of readings over the whole history of theology can only point the interested reader in some useful directions. Many of the books listed here have extended bibliographies that can lead on to further reading.

General

Some reference works

The Westminster Dictionary of Church History, ed. by Jerald C. Brauer. Philadelphia: Westminster Press, 1971.

The Oxford Dictionary of the Christian Church, 2nd ed., ed. by F. L. Cross and Elizabeth A. Livingstone. Oxford: Oxford University Press, 1974.

Eerdmans' Handbook to the History of Christianity, ed. by Tim Dowley. Grand Rapids: Wm. B. Eerdmans Publishing Co., 1977. This work is theologically quite conservative but attractively illustrated and accessible in style and layout.

General histories of Christianity

Paul Johnson, *A History of Christianity.* New York: Atheneum Publishers, 1976. A somewhat polemic history by a gifted British journalist.

Martin E. Marty, *A Short History of Christianity.* Cleveland: World Publishing Co./Meridian Books, 1959. Well written and on an introductory level.

Williston Walker, *A History of the Christian Church,* 4th ed. New York: Charles Scribner's Sons, 1985. Updated since its original publication many years ago, and perhaps still the standard source.

Histories of theology

Hubert Cunliffe-Jones and Benjamin Drewery, eds., *A History of Christian Doctrine.* Philadelphia: Fortress Press, 1980. A collection of chapters by leading scholars in various fields, this is somewhat more advanced than the other books listed.

Jaroslav Pelikan, *Jesus Through the Centuries.* New York: Harper & Row, 1985. Not exactly a survey history, but wonderfully readable and in a class by itself as an intellectual *tour de force.*

William C. Placher, *A History of Christian Theology.* Philadelphia: Westminster Press, 1983.

Linwood Urban, *A Short History of Christian Thought.* New York: Oxford University Press, 1986.

Collections of readings

Colman J. Barry, ed., *Readings in Church History,* 3 vols. in 1. Westminster, Md.: Christian Classics, 1985. An anthology that focuses more on institutional history than this book does.

The many volumes of the *Library of Christian Classics,* published by The Westminster Press, and the *Classics of Western Spirituality,* now being published by Paulist Press, represent the best general collections of readings in primary sources.

The Early Church

Henry Chadwick, *The Early Church.* Baltimore: Penguin Books, 1967. A good introduction to the history of the period.

Jaroslav Pelikan, *The Emergence of the Catholic Tradition.* Chicago: University of Chicago Press, 1971. The first volume of Pelikan's *The Christian Tradition:* difficult for a reader without some knowledge of the period, but a magisterial work.

Gnosticism

Hans Jonas, *The Gnostic Religion.* Boston: Beacon Press, 1958. Written before recently discovered texts were available, this remains the most intellectually suggestive study.

Elaine Pagels, *The Gnostic Gospels.* New York: Random House/Vintage Books, 1981. A good introduction.

Kurt Rudolph, *Gnosis,* tr. by Robert M. Wilson. New York: Harper & Row, 1983. The most complete scholarly survey.

Apologists

Gerald Bray, *Holiness and the Will of God.* Atlanta: John Knox Press, 1979. On Tertullian.

Henry Chadwick, *Early Christian Thought and the Classical Tradition.* New York: Oxford University Press, 1966.

Charles N. Cochrane, *Christianity and Classical Culture.* New York: Oxford University Press, 1944. Difficult, but still a masterful work.

John Ferguson, *Clement of Alexandria.* Boston: Twayne Publishers, 1974.

Joseph W. Trigg, *Origen.* Atlanta: John Knox Press, 1983.

The Trinity and Christology

Edmund J. Fortman, *The Triune God.* Philadelphia: Westminster Press, 1972.

Aloys Grillmeier, *Christ in Christian Tradition,* tr. by John Bowden. Atlanta: John Knox Press, 1975.

J. N. D. Kelly, *Early Christian Doctrine.* New York: Harper & Row, 1978. The most balanced, thorough discussion.

Robert Payne, *The Holy Fire.* Crestwood, N.Y.: St. Vladimir's Seminary Press, 1980. Wonderful biographies of the church fathers.

Frances M. Young, *From Nicaea to Chalcedon.* Philadelphia: Fortress Press, 1983. A useful survey of the current state of research.

The Eastern Church

Harry J. Magoulias, *Byzantine Christianity.* Detroit: Wayne State University Press, 1982.

John Meyendorff, *Byzantine Theology.* Bronx, N.Y.: Fordham University Press, 1974. Probably the best introduction.

———, *Christ in Eastern Christian Thought.* Washington, D.C.: Corpus Books, 1969.

Jaroslav Pelikan, *The Spirit of Eastern Christendom* (*The Christian Tradition,* vol. 2). Chicago: University of Chicago Press, 1974. Perhaps the most valuable of all the volumes of Pelikan's history of doctrine.

Alexander Schmemann, *The Historical Road of Eastern Orthodoxy.* New York: Holt, Rinehart, & Winston, 1963.

Augustine

Peter Brown, *Augustine of Hippo.* Berkeley, Calif.: University of California Press, 1967. A quite wonderful intellectual biography.

Warren Thomas Smith, *Augustine.* Atlanta: John Knox Press, 1980. A good introductory biography.

The Middle Ages

General Surveys

F. C. Copleston, *A History of Medieval Philosophy.* New York: Harper & Row, 1972.

David Knowles, *The Evolution of Medieval Thought.* New York: Helicon Press, 1962.

Jaroslav Pelikan, *The Growth of Medieval Theology* (*The Christian Tradition,* vol. 3). Chicago: University of Chicago Press, 1978.

Jeffrey Burton Russell, *A History of Medieval Christianity.* New York: Thomas Y. Crowell, 1968.

R. W. Southern, *Western Society and the Church in the Middle Ages.* Baltimore: Penguin Books, 1970.

Walter Ullmann, *A History of Political Thought: The Middle Ages.* Baltimore: Penguin Books, 1965.

Issues in the Earlier Period

Peter Brown, *The Cult of the Saints.* Chicago: University of Chicago Press, 1981.

Jean Leclercq, *The Love of Learning and the Desire for God,* tr. by Catharine Misrahi. Bronx, N.Y.: Fordham University Press, 1985. On the monastic tradition.

A. J. Macdonald, *Berengar and the Reform of Sacramental Doctrine.* Merrick, N.Y.: Richwood Publishing Co., 1977.

John Marenbon, *Early Medieval Philosophy.* Boston: Routledge & Kegan Paul, 1983.

The High Middle Ages

Frederick Copleston, *Aquinas.* Baltimore: Penguin Books, 1956.

Etienne Gilson, *Reason and Revelation in the Middle Ages.* New York: Charles Scribner's Sons, 1938. Sets out many of the crucial issues in less than a hundred pages.

Brian Tierney, *The Crisis of Church and State 1050–1300.* Englewood

Cliffs, N.J.: Prentice-Hall, 1964. A collection of primary texts, but with fine editorial introductions.

Julius R. Weinberg, *A Short History of Medieval Philosophy*. Princeton, N.J.: Princeton University Press, 1964.

The Later Middle Ages

Gordon Leff, *The Dissolution of the Medieval Outlook*. New York: Harper & Row, 1976.

Francis Oakley, *The Western Church in the Later Middle Ages*. Ithaca, N.Y.: Cornell University Press, 1979.

Heiko A. Oberman, *Forerunners of the Reformation*. Philadelphia: Fortress Press, 1981.

Steven Ozment, *The Age of Reform 1250–1550*. New Haven, Conn.: Yale University Press, 1980.

Index